Art for All Seasons

The art ideas in this book are centered around an element of a season, the weather or a holiday. Patterns and step-by-step directions are included where needed.

- Printing
- Drawing
- Collage
- 3-D Constructions
- Greeting Card Ideas
- Sponge Painting
- Pop-up Activities
- Murals
- And more!

Congratulations on your purchase of some of the finest teaching materials in the world.

Entire contents copyright ©1993 by EVAN-MOOR CORP.
18 Lower Ragsdale Drive, Monterey, CA 93940-5746

Author: Jo Ellen Moore
Editor: Joy Evans

Original editions:
Fall Art Ideas, © 1986 by Evan-Moor Corp.
Winter Art Ideas, © 1986 by Evan-Moor Corp.
Spring Art Ideas, © 1986 by Evan-Moor Corp.

Evan-Moor
EDUCATIONAL PUBLISHERS

Fall

Drawing Trees for Any Season

Choose one picture from each section. Draw large enough to
fill your page. Create an interesting tree. . .or forest of trees.
Use your own imagination to create other types of trees.

Trunks

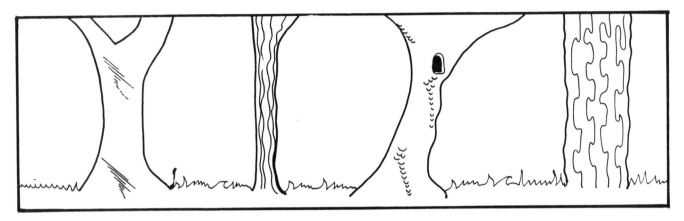

Branches

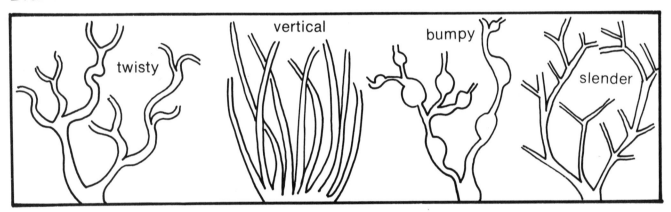

Foliage

Be a brave soul and draw with your students. If you will
demonstrate on the chalkboard or overhead projector, your
class will be more confident in attempting unfamiliar scenes.
Everyone needs to learn that drawing is something we
investigate together; there is no right or wrong way to do it.

                   Seasonal Art

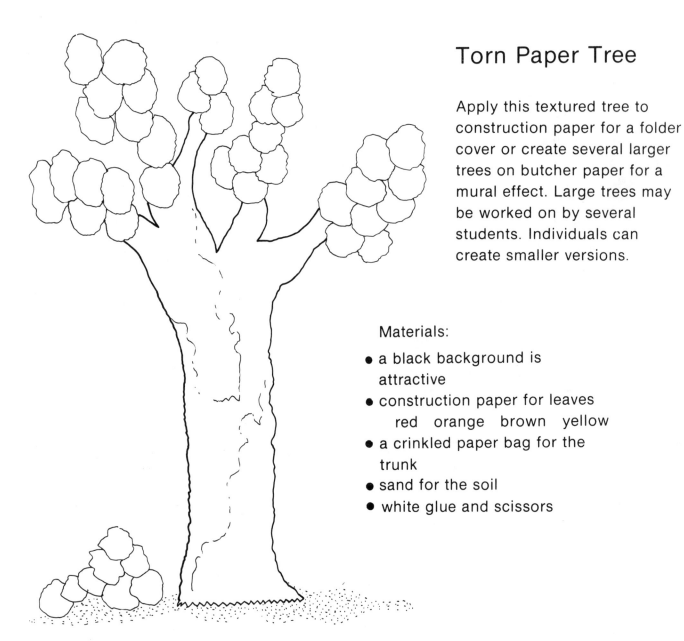

Torn Paper Tree

Apply this textured tree to construction paper for a folder cover or create several larger trees on butcher paper for a mural effect. Large trees may be worked on by several students. Individuals can create smaller versions.

Materials:

- a black background is attractive
- construction paper for leaves
    red   orange   brown   yellow
- a crinkled paper bag for the trunk
- sand for the soil
- white glue and scissors

Steps to follow:

1. Flatten out the crinkled paper bag and cut out a trunk shape. Branches may be cut as part of the trunk or added separately.

   Allow some branches to buckle out. You can twist some branches before pasting down.

   Paste the trunk and branches to the background.

2. Tear off "roundish" pieces of construction paper to be leaves. Alternate the colors and paste to the branches. Begin at the lower end. Overlap each piece.

   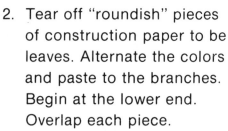

3. Smear white glue along the bottom of the picture. Sprinkle sand on the glue to form the soil. Let the picture dry.

Seasonal Art

Sponge Print Trees for Each Season

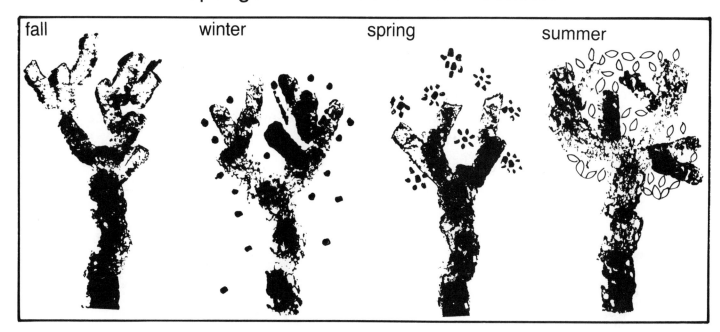

fall   winter   spring   summer

These trees require large easel paint paper so that the branches can spread out. The finished trees may also create an effective mural to brighten your classroom during any season.

You may paint only the trees representing one season or all four trees to show the changes in each season.

Materials:
- large newsprint
- tempera paint
  - brown   yellow
  - orange   green
  - red   pink
- sponges
- paper towels

Steps to follow:
1. Cut the sponges to the sizes and shapes you need.
   - leaf shape
   - snowballs
   - rectangles—trunk, branches
   - blossom shapes
   - flower centers

   Pencil erasers are also useful in printing details.

2. Place the paint in shallow dishes.
   Dip the desired sponge shape in paint to coat the sponge bottom. Blot lightly on paper towel to remove the excess paint.

3. Print on newsprint, beginning with the tree trunk and branches.

4. Add leaves, snow, flowers, etc. choosing whatever is appropriate to the season being represented.

Wonderful Ways With Fall Leaves

Gather fall leaves in various shapes and sizes. Designs will be more effective if you have a good variety to choose from.

Explore with many combinations of colored paper and arrangements of leaves and colors to discover which are most pleasing.

Here are several different ways to put your leaves to work!

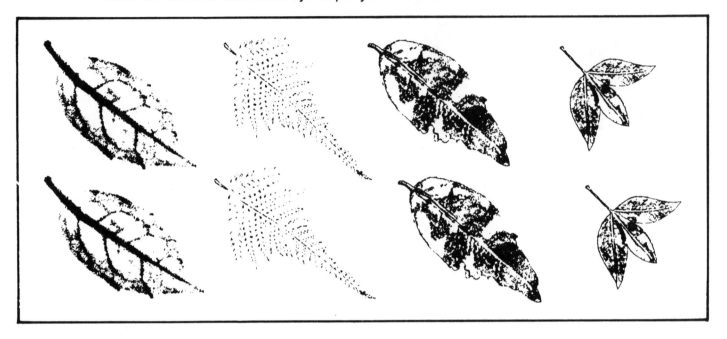

Prints	Rubbings	Stencils
Lay the leaf on a piece of old newspaper. Paint the leaf back with a coat of tempera. Press the leaf onto construction paper. Peel off the leaf and see your print.	Arrange one leaf at a time under a piece of colored paper. Rub over the top with the flat side of a crayon. Choose another shape leaf and repeat. Remember, overlapping of leaves and colors can be effective.	Trace your favorite leaf shape on a piece of tagboard. Use an Exacto knife to cut out the shape to form your stencil. Use the flat side of a crayon for an overall color or press in from the edge of the stencil with a crayon point for a more decorative effect.

Seasonal Art

Apple Art

This lesson is a natural accompaniment to a unit on various types of apples. These are colorful when used alone, but may also be assembled on a bulletin board for a striking effect.

Materials:
- Black construction paper square
- Red, green or yellow square— slightly smaller
- White square—even smaller
- Scraps of brown (stem) and green (leaf)
- Scissors, paste, black crayon.

Steps to follow:

1. Fold red, yellow or green paper in half. Cut on fold.

2. Fold and cut the white paper.

3. Paste the white shape on the colored shape. Use black crayon to add seeds.

4. Cut a stem from brown and a leaf from green.

5. Arrange all pieces on the black square. Paste pieces down.

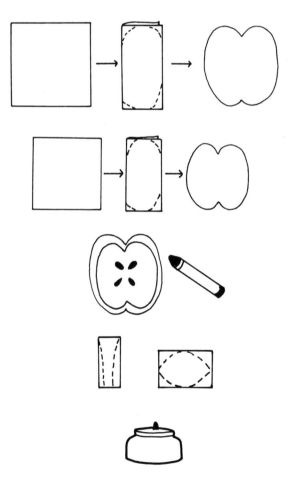

Apple Prints

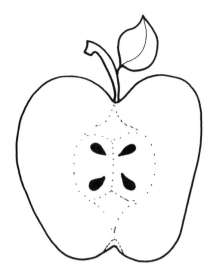

Use the simple design of a cut apple as the theme for this print. You can guarantee dramatic results by controlling the color combinations you offer students.

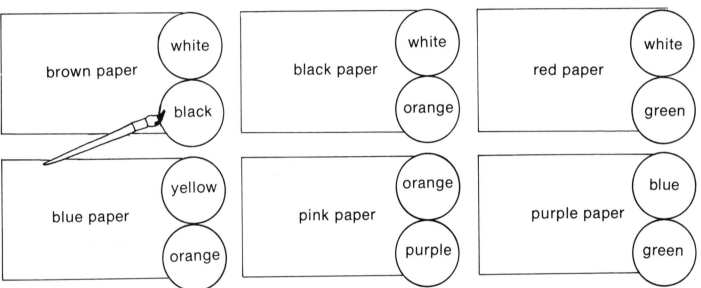

brown paper	white / black
black paper	white / orange
red paper	white / green
blue paper	yellow / orange
pink paper	orange / purple
purple paper	blue / green

Encourage students to try a variety of designs:
Repeating the same pattern for the whole line.
Alternating right side up and upside down.
Random placement.
Vertical lines, instead of horizontal.
Print only the border, leaving the center empty.

Steps to follow:
1. Dip apple into a shallow dish of paint.
2. Press carefully on paper.

You will have better results if the children practice on newsprint or old newspapers first. They can then create a final design on construction paper or butcher paper.

Seasonal Art

Scarecrow

Would this fellow scare the crows away or would he hide birdseed in his pockets as a special treat for his "feathered" friends?

Materials:
- Reproduce the pattern on the following page.
- Ice cream sticks
- Glue, crayons, scissors
- Brown construction paper
- Green paper scraps

Steps to follow:

1. Color the pattern pieces.

2. Cut out all pieces.

3. **Follow the folding instructions printed on the pattern pieces.**

4. Use glue to secure:
   a. ice cream stick in fold to form arms.
   b. head on shoulders.
   c. bird on stick.
   d. scarecrow to the brown construction paper.

5. Use green paper scraps (or a green crayon) to create the crop your scarecrow is protecting.

Scarecrow Pattern

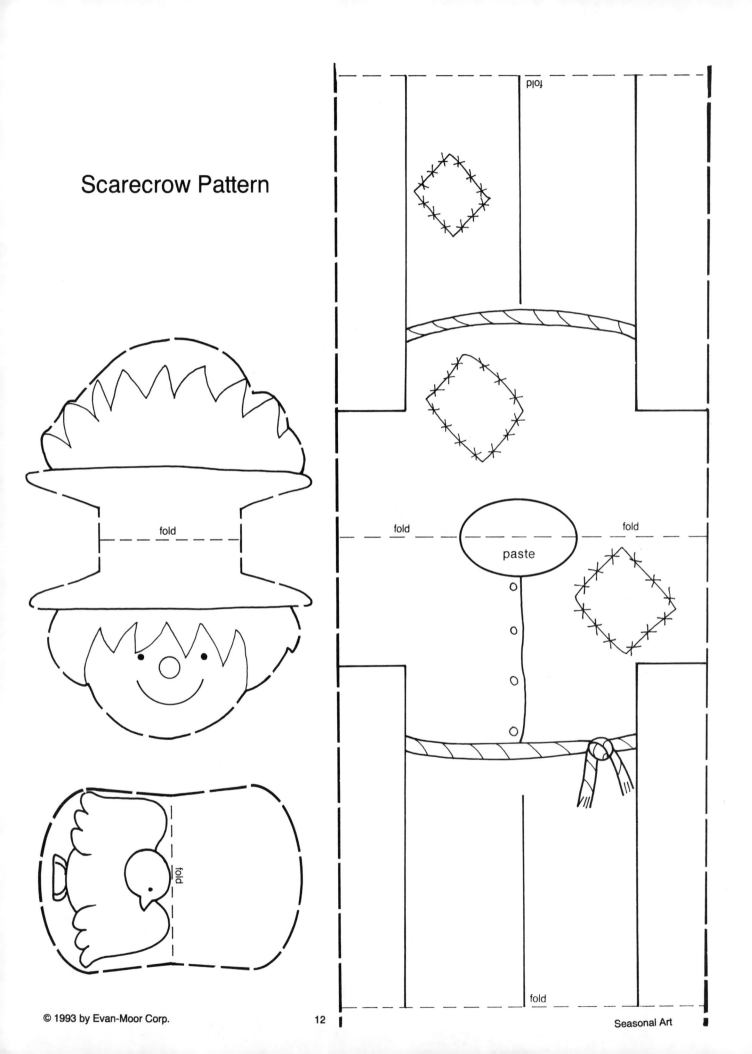

fold

fold

paste

fold

fold

fold

fold

12

Seasonal Art

Watch the Seasons Turn

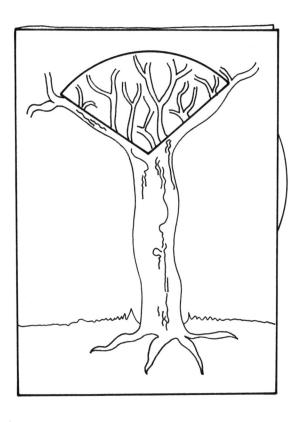

This project provides a stimulus to discussion long after it is finished. Students can spin the wheel and watch the seasons change to help reinforce facts learned in science class.

Materials:
- reproduce the patterns on the following pages.
- paper fasteners
- crayons or felt markers
- scissors
- paste

Steps to follow:
1. Prepare the pattern pieces. Cut on dotted lines. Fold on solid lines.

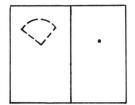

2. Insert a paper fastener through the dot on the wheel and then through the dot on the cover page.

3. Close the cover. Put a dot of paste on the two outside corners.

4. Sketch the tree trunk on the outside. Add details with crayons or felt pens.

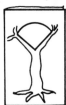

5. Turn wheel to the first section. Begin by drawing branches with fall leaves in the window. Turn the wheel until the fall branches disappear. Now show branches with all the leaves gone. The bare branches could have a layer of snow.
Turn the wheel again and draw branches bursting with spring buds and new leaves. Finally, turn the wheel and draw branches full of green leaves for summer.

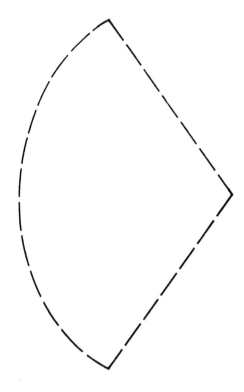

Wheel Pattern

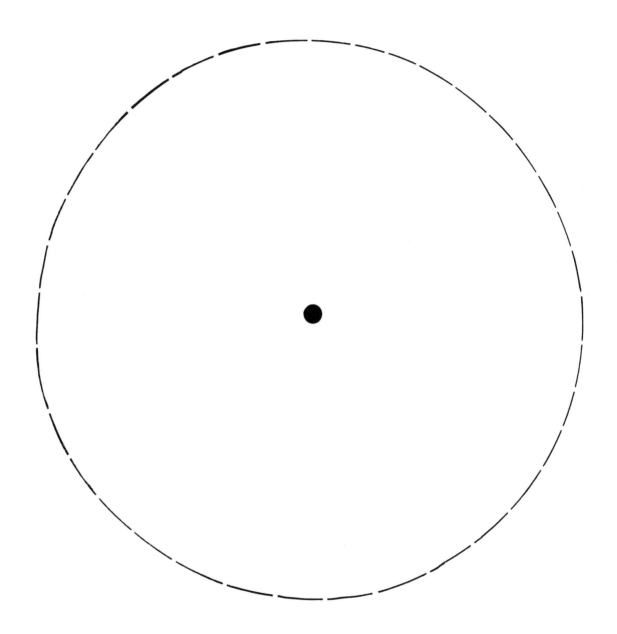

15 Seasonal Art

A Pop-Up ABC Book for Fall

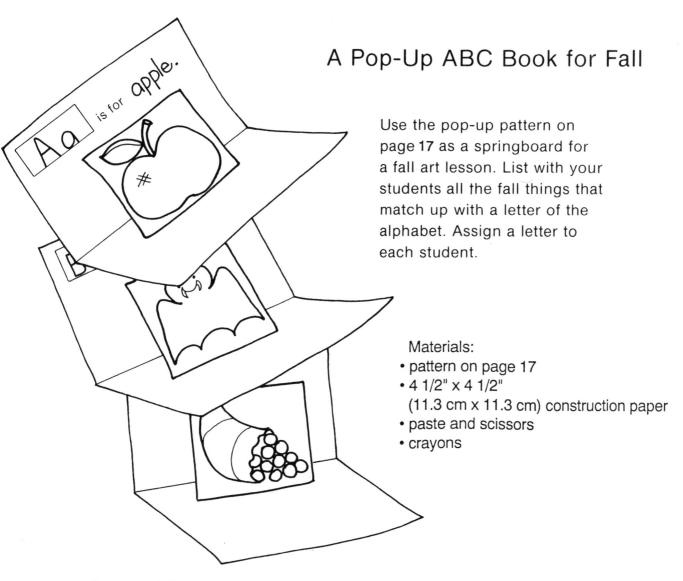

Use the pop-up pattern on page **17** as a springboard for a fall art lesson. List with your students all the fall things that match up with a letter of the alphabet. Assign a letter to each student.

Materials:
- pattern on page 17
- 4 1/2" x 4 1/2" (11.3 cm x 11.3 cm) construction paper
- paste and scissors
- crayons

Steps to follow:

1. Give each student a copy of the pop-up pattern. Cut and fold the form together.

2. Give each student a white sheet of construction paper 4½" X 4½". Draw a picture of their fall word on this paper.

3. Students should draw a fall background on their form.

4. Cut out and paste the illustration to the pop-up tab.

These pages can be pasted back to back to create a class book.

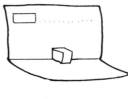

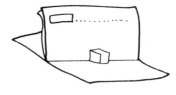

Pop-up Pattern. Fold, cut and push the tab to the inside.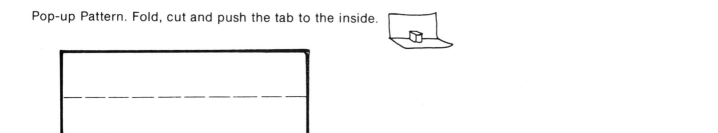

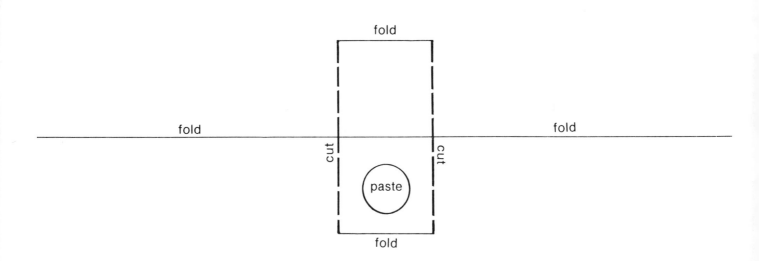

fold

fold   fold

cut   cut

paste

fold

Seasonal Art

Pumpkins in the Field

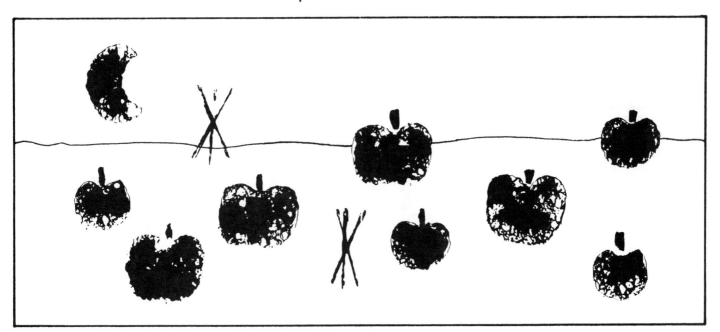

These pumpkins appear to glow in the dark. Fill your pumpkin patch with sponge prints on a dark background.

Materials:
- tempera—green, white, orange
- sponges
- cardboard strips
- large dark blue construction paper

Steps to follow:

1. Cut sponge pieces into pumpkin and moon shapes.

2. Pour puddles of paint in saucers or coffee can lids.

3. Dab the pumpkin sponge into orange paint and print on the blue paper. Repeat several times.

4. Place the moon sponge into white paint and print.

5. Dip the edge of a cardboard strip in green paint. Print in overlapping lines.

6. Use a shorter cardboard strip dipped in green to create stems for your pumpkins.

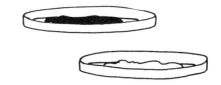

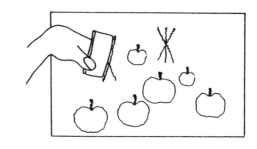

 Seasonal Art

Drawing Jack-O'-Lanterns

Jack-o'-lanterns are just like people, no two are exactly alike. They are easy to draw and many variations are possible. Draw a lot...make each and every one something special.

Some shape and face ideas:

Give your jack-o'-lantern the impression of roundness by drawing curving groove lines.

Paper Maché Jack-O-Lanterns

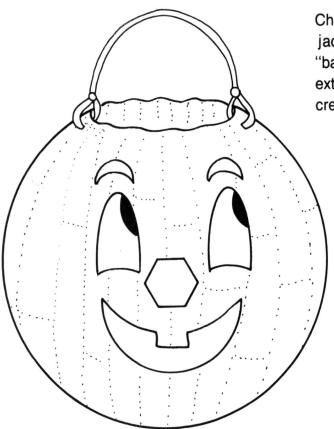

Children are delighted with their jack-o-lantern trick or treat "baskets." It takes a little time and extra effort, but it's well worth it to create a very special project.

Materials:
- balloons
- milk cartons—school-sized containers work well
- paste—wallpaper paste, liquid starch or white glue thinned with water
- newspaper strips—about 1″ by 6″ (2.5 cm x 15 cm)
- masking tape

Steps to follow:

1. Cover work areas with several layers of newspaper. (Plan where the project will sit during drying time.)

2. Prepare the balloon. Blow the balloon up, tie the end, push the end through a slit in the milk carton, and tape firmly. The milk carton serves as a stand while you work.

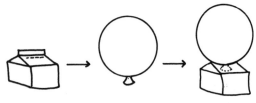

3. Cover the balloon. Dip the strips of newspaper in the paste. Wipe against the edge of the dish to remove excess. Place on the balloon.

Overlap pieces slightly, covering the entire balloon with a single layer of "pasty" paper. Let it dry thoroughly.

4. Repeat step 3 until the balloon has 3 or 4 layers of paper.

5. Paint your pumpkin with orange tempera. Let it dry thoroughly.

6. When the paint is dry, cut the balloon loose from the milk carton to release air from the balloon. Pull balloon pieces out of the pumpkin form.

7. Sit the pumpkin upright and paint your jack-o-lantern's face.

8. Let it dry; add a yarn handle. You're all set to go trick-or-treating.

 Seasonal Art

Positive-Negative Pumpkins

Use orange and black construction paper to create Halloween jack o'lanterns.

This can be put together to form a quilt-like display showing the variety of designs produced by your students.

The designs could also be used as a border for a colorful bulletin board displaying Halloween stories and poems.

Materials:

- an orange construction paper

- a black construction paper rectangle, ½ the size of the orange

- scissors and paste

Steps to follow:

1. Lay the black paper on the right side of the orange.

   Draw ½ of a jack o'lantern with pencil or yellow crayon.

2. Cut on the pencil lines. Lift up the main pumpkin shape and place it on the left side. Paste the shapes in place.

Seasonal Art

Black Cat on a Fence

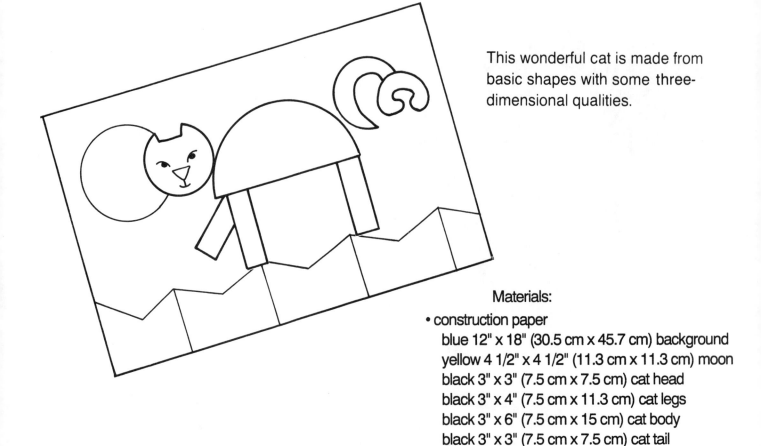

This wonderful cat is made from basic shapes with some three-dimensional qualities.

Materials:

- construction paper
  blue 12" x 18" (30.5 cm x 45.7 cm) background
  yellow 4 1/2" x 4 1/2" (11.3 cm x 11.3 cm) moon
  black 3" x 3" (7.5 cm x 7.5 cm) cat head
  black 3" x 4" (7.5 cm x 11.3 cm) cat legs
  black 3" x 6" (7.5 cm x 15 cm) cat body
  black 3" x 3" (7.5 cm x 7.5 cm) cat tail
- scissors, paste, crayons

Steps to follow:

1. Cut out a large yellow circle. Paste to the blue background.

2. Cut the black paper to form the cat.

3. Lay the cat pieces on the blue paper and draw the fence line with orange or yellow crayon.

4. Paste the cat's body parts in place on the blue paper.

It's fun to paste an accordian strip spacer behind the cat's head for a 3-D look.
Pull the end of the tail out and down to complete the picture.

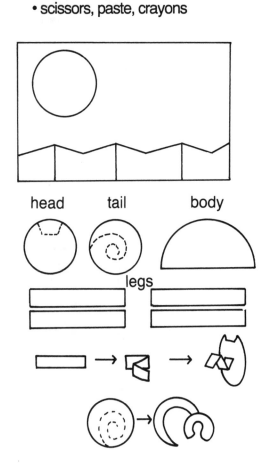

Spider on a Web

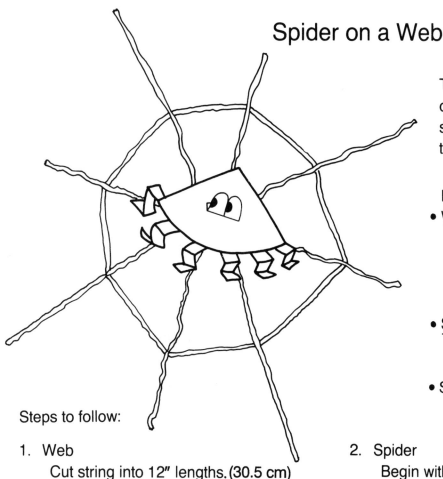

This web can be taped in the corner of a doorway for a real surprise for friends who come to trick or treat.

Materials:
- Web
    - white string
    - liquid starch (in small saucers)
    - wax paper
- Spider
    - black construction paper
    - scraps of colored paper
- Scissors, glue

Steps to follow:

1. Web

    Cut string into 12″ lengths. (30.5 cm) Each student gets 6 lengths and a sheet of wax paper.

    Dip each strip of string in the liquid starch and arrange on the wax paper. Begin with an X.

    Allow the web to dry completely.

2. Spider

    Begin with a 5″ (15 cm) black square. Round the corners to create a circle.
    Fold the circle in quarters.
    Open and cut to the center on one fold line.
    Lap over two edges and paste to form a cone shape.
    Cut out eight legs from black paper.
    Fold each leg into quarters.
    Open and paste one edge of each leg to the black cone.
    Refold legs so they bend back and forth.
    Add eyes (from scraps of colored paper) that stand up.

    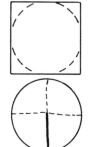

    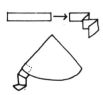

    Paste eyes to the spider.
    Put dabs of glue on the spider's feet and place him on his web.

    After the glue dries you can tape the web in a corner of a doorway.

Seasonal Art

Bats

These bats are easy to develop into a successful art lesson for your class. Make them in several sizes and use them to enhance an October bulletin board.

Materials:
- black construction paper (4½" x 6" is an effective size) (11.3 cm x 15 cm)
- scissors
- hole punch
- crayons
- blue construction paper

Steps to follow:
1. Fold the black paper in half. Draw the bat outline with pencil (see picture) and cut along the pencil lines.
2. Punch holes for the eyes. Draw the mouth and fangs with yellow crayon.
3. Paste the bats to blue paper. They now have blue eyes! Add other nighttime or Halloween items to the paper.
   harvest moon
   black outlines of trees
   witch on broom
   ghosts drifting in front of the moon

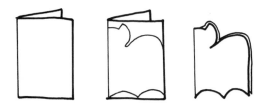

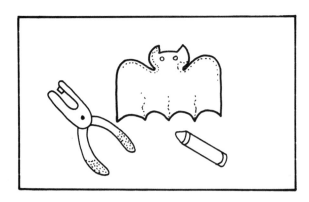

Skeleton

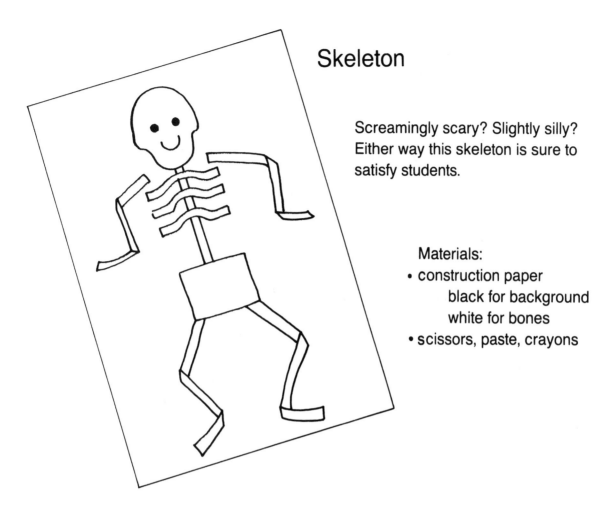

Screamingly scary? Slightly silly? Either way this skeleton is sure to satisfy students.

Materials:
- construction paper
    - black for background
    - white for bones
- scissors, paste, crayons

Steps to follow:

1. Cut white paper to form:

skull and pelvis

ribs and spine

legs and arms

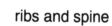

2. Trim the skull on the fold. Add eye sockets and mouth with a black crayon.

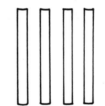

3. Paste the various body parts on the black paper. Begin with the skull and spine. Add the ribs by putting paste on each end and letting the center of the strip buckle up. Bend the leg and arm strips at the joints before pasting down.

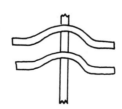

Paper Bag Masks

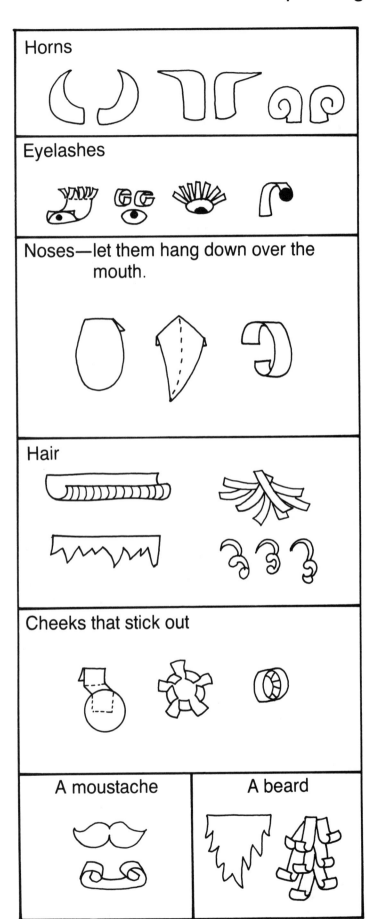

Horns

Eyelashes

Noses—let them hang down over the mouth.

Hair

Cheeks that stick out

A moustache   **A beard**

Turn your students loose to create their own wonderful masks for Halloween. These can be simple or made elaborate by adding all your "junk" for extra sparkle.

Materials:
• large brown grocery bags
• scraps of paper
• box of "junk" (ribbon, buttons, pipe cleaners, etc.)

Steps to follow:
1. Cut the sturdy mask shape from a grocery bag. You can cut several from one bag.

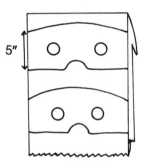

5″

Cut eyes to suit each student.

2. Staple leftover strips of paper bag to the edge of the mask to create a headband.

3. Now make all those imaginative features that make the mask uniquely yours.

   Do any coloring first.

   Black outlining is very effective.

4. Use scraps or "junk" to add special features.

Pumpkin Seed Smile
Who Is It?

Materials:
- large construction paper (any color)
- circle of construction paper in the same color for the mouth
- scissors, glue, crayons
- pumpkin seeds

A few quick and easy steps are all that you need to create these spectacular "smilers."

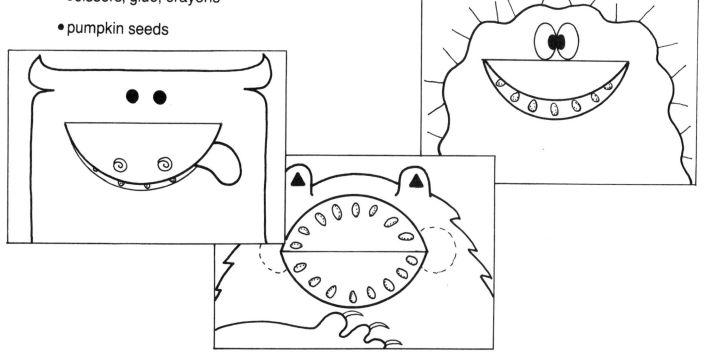

Steps to follow:

1. Fold the circle in half. Glue the pumpkin seeds in a ring around the inside.

2. Close the circle back in half. Paste the half circle in the center of the large construction paper.

3. Now use crayons to finish this fellow's face.

   Who is it anyway?

Seasonal Art

Peek-a-Boo Ghost

Lift up the ghost flap and see who is there!

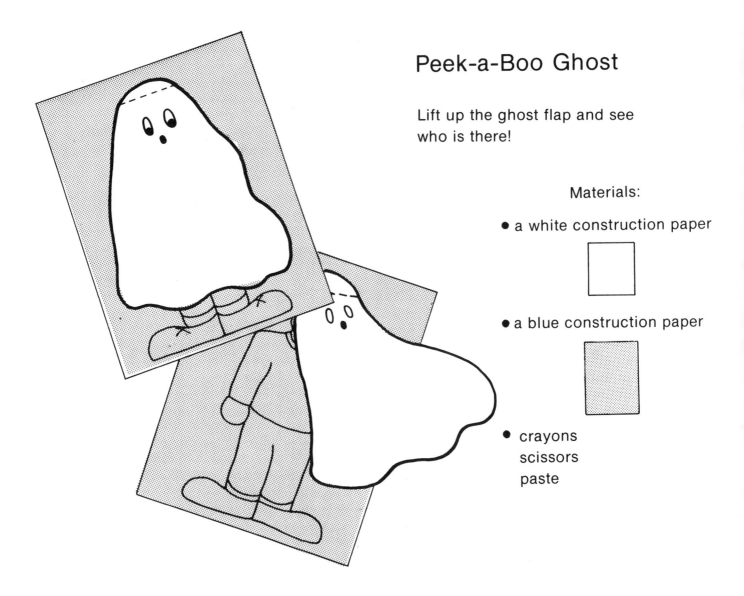

Materials:

- a white construction paper

- a blue construction paper

- crayons
  scissors
  paste

Steps to follow:

1. Cut out a ghost shape from the white paper.

   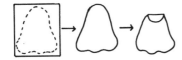

   Fold down the top edge.

2. Paste the fold of the ghost to the blue paper.

3. Outline the ghost with black crayon *on the blue paper.*

4. Lift up the ghost and draw someone. Stay inside the ghost shape except for the feet.

5. Use crayons to draw a spooky background.

   Crayon in eyes and a mouth for your ghost.

Seasonal Art

See-Through Ghosts

A set of these spooky folks would dangle nicely from your light fixtures or in your windows.

Materials:
- newspaper
- wax paper
- scraps of construction paper
- scissors
- iron
- string or clear fish line

Steps to follow:

1. Place 2 sheets of wax paper together and cut out a ghost shape.

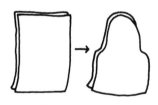

2. Cut eyes and a mouth from construction paper. Lay them between the sheets of wax paper.

3. Place the wax paper between 2 sheets of newspaper. Press with a *warm* iron. Teacher may want to do this step.

4. Now you are ready to fringe (or rip) the bottom of your ghost. This will help make the ghost look like it is flying.

5. Punch a hole in the ghost and hang it with a piece of string or the fish line.

Seasonal Art

Pop-Up Halloween Goblin

This pop-up pattern is sure to inspire students to create wonderful spooks and goblins ready to creep in the Halloween night.

Reproduce the pattern on page **31** . Do the cut and fold directions together.

Have the students open and close their pop-up goblin mouth many times before beginning their drawings. When they can see what they want to make, they may begin drawing using crayons or felt markers.

The finished product may be pasted to construction paper for added strength and durability.

Steps to follow:

1. Fold on 1.

2. Cut on solid line.

3. Fold on 2

4. Fold on 3

5. Open the paper and reverse folds 2 and 3 by pushing them to the inside.

6. Close and press the folds again. Pinch and pull the pop up portion from the inside.

Pop-Up Halloween Goblin Pattern

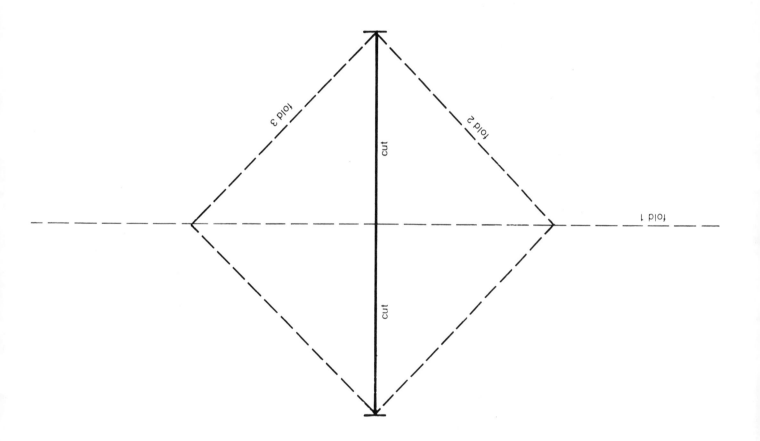

Seasonal Art

Pull Through Monster Face

This activitiy can be large or small, elaborate or simple...

Students may draw with crayons or felt markers. If you want to take more time, students can use paper scraps to make the outside design appear three-dimensional.

Each student will need:

- two sheets of white construction paper

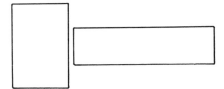

- crayons or felt markers
- scissors

Steps to follow:

1. Cut two slits in the first sheet of paper.

2. Thread the long strip through the slits.

3. Draw the outside part of your monster's head.

4. Draw the first face on the strip. Pull the strip until you reach a clean space. Create another face. Continue moving the strip and draw–ing new faces until you run out of room.

5. Now...share your spooky expressions with a friend.

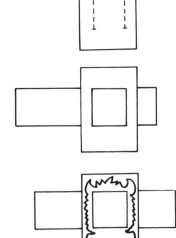

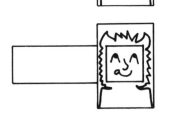

Seasonal Art

Paper Doll Witch

Dress your witch for any occasion. What does a well-dressed witch wear?

swim suit	raincoat
party dress	pajamas
running suit	jumpsuit
wedding dress	
Halloween costume	

Reproduce the paper doll pattern on page **34** .
Use construction paper or tagboard.

Steps to follow:

1. Color and cut out the paper doll form. Tape the paper doll to the window.

2. Tape white paper over it, so you can see the doll shape through the paper. Draw the piece of clothing to fit the witch.

3. Color the clothing and add tabs so the clothes will stay on the paper doll. Cut out the clothing.

4. Dress the witch in her new outfit and explain to a friend why you made that choice.

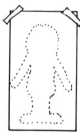

Seasonal Art

Witch Paper Doll Pattern

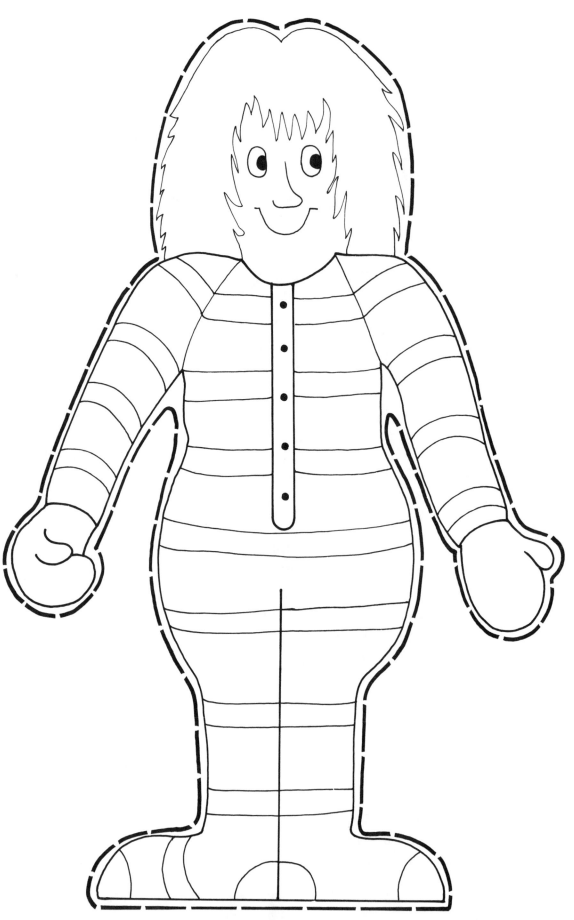

Seasonal Art

A Dancing Witch

This little witch is perfect for hanging in the window to welcome Halloween.

Materials:
- white construction paper
  black construction paper
  orange construction paper
- brass paper fasteners
- crayons
- scissors
- glue or paste

Steps to follow:

1.

Cut out the head piece first. Cut other pieces to match that size.
Cut a round head and hand from the white construction paper.

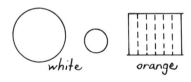

Add hair from orange paper strips. Draw the face with crayons.

2.

Round corners of a black paper square to create a circle. Fold the circle in half and cut on the fold. One half becomes the witch's cape, the other half can be cut to form the hat and boots. (See the illustration.)

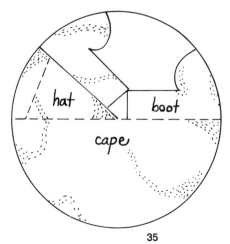

3.

Cut an orange pumpkin to go in the witch's hand. Paste the hand and pumpkin to the body.

Use paper fasteners to connect the head and boots to the body. Fold the cape around.
Hang the witch by a string attached to her hat.

 Seasonal Art

A Haunted House

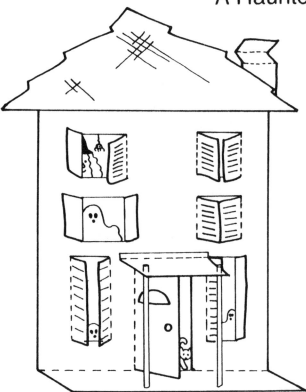

Imaginations can really run wild with this project. It is simple enough for primary children to enjoy, or can become complicated enough to stimulate any fifth or sixth grader. These houses may be mounted on a bulletin board as motivation for writing "spooky" stories.

Materials:
- construction paper
    - black
    - orange
    - white
    - brown
    - assorted scraps
- paste, scissors, crayons
- extras
    - straws (porch supports)
    - cotton (cobwebs)
    - Exacto knife (for cutting open doors and windows)

Steps to follow:

1. The house is created from an 8" x 12" (20.5 cm x 30.5 cm) sheet of black paper. Fold up the front porch. Outline windows and doors with yellow crayons.

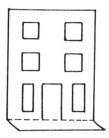

2. Use the Exacto knife or scissors to cut open the door flap and window shutters. Paste a sheet of white paper on the back of the house. Now when you open each window you can draw a surprise inside.
   A witch peeking out.
   A ghost watching you.
   A black cat sitting with his back arched.
   A spider spinning his web.

3. The roof is a brown paper triangle. It needs to be crooked. Outline it with black and add cross hatching. Paste it to the top of the house.

4. The chimney is a red paper rectangle folded back and forth. Paste it behind the roof.

5. Extras:
   Add a yellow moon peeking over the roof.
   Create a front porch using a black paper flap and straws.

         Seasonal Art

Draw a Ship

This lesson could be adapted for Colombus Day or as a part of a unit on the Mayflower.

Follow the drawing steps.

Draw the water line.
Add the basic boat
shape.

Add the masts.
Put on a railing and port
holes.

Draw the sails full of
wind.

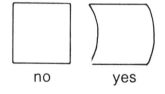

no   yes

Add the final touches.
   flags
   lines
   crow's nest
Create a background for
your ship.

                   Seasonal Art

Columbus Sails!

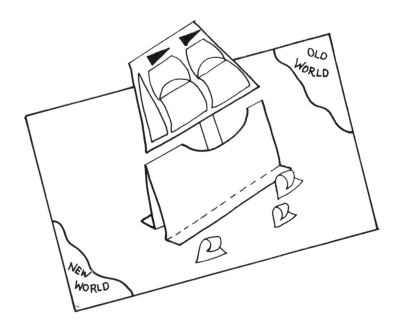

Create a scene that brings the Columbus story to life for your students. (This could also become the Mayflower.)

Materials:
- large blue construction paper
- scraps of blue paper for the waves
- brown and white construction paper
- tongue depressor

Steps to follow:
1. Fold the brown paper and cut on the fold as shown. Turn up the bottom edge on the front and back.
2. Fold the white paper and trim as shown.
3. Paste the tongue depressor inside the brown paper. Paste the white paper around the top of the stick.
4. Draw the sails and mast on the white paper. Add flags, lines, and a crow's nest if you wish.
5. Paste the base of the ship to the blue paper. Add curled paper waves around the ship.
6. Use crayons or brown paper scraps to add the Old World and the New World. (Be sure your ship is sailing in the right direction!)

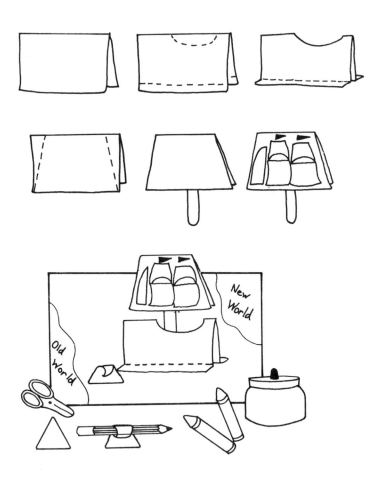

Draw The Crew
of the Santa Maria

The Santa Maria had 40 men in the crew. Christopher Columbus was in charge but there was also a Captain for the ship. The crew had many jobs. There was a doctor, a carpenter, a clerk and many others that kept the ship in order and on course to the New World.

Materials:
- drawing paper—12″ X 18″ (30.5 cm x 45.7 cm)
- colored pencils

Steps to follow:
Draw the basic shapes.
What did they wear?
Where are they?
You might draw them on the ship.
Show them working the sails or perched in the crow's nest.
Perhaps you will show the crew having landed in the New World.

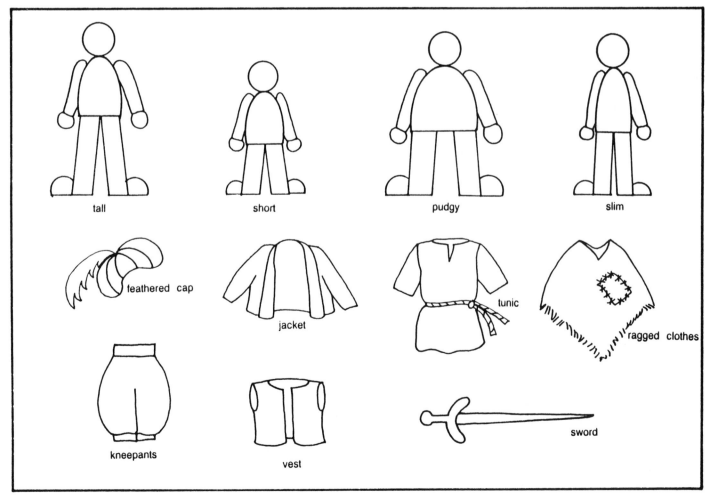

tall   short   pudgy   slim

feathered cap   jacket   tunic   ragged clothes

kneepants   vest   sword

Torn Paper Cornucopia

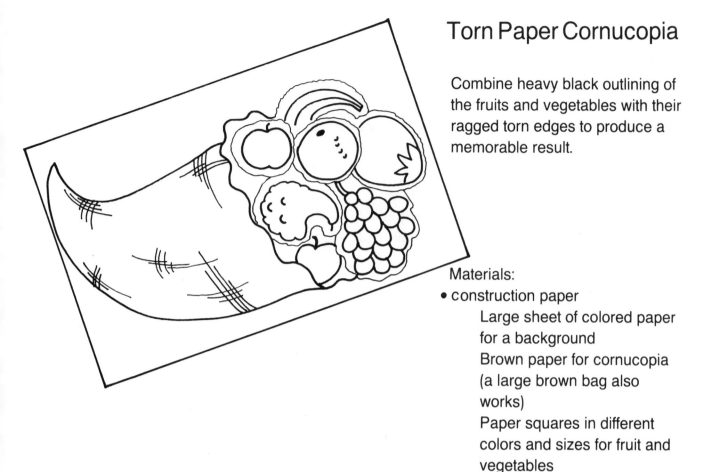

Combine heavy black outlining of the fruits and vegetables with their ragged torn edges to produce a memorable result.

Materials:
- construction paper

    Large sheet of colored paper for a background

    Brown paper for cornucopia (a large brown bag also works)

    Paper squares in different colors and sizes for fruit and vegetables
- black felt pens for outlining
- scissors and paste

Steps to follow:

1. Design and cut out the cornucopia. Paste it to the background. Add cross-hatching and outlining details with black marker.

2. Draw selected fruits and vegetables on the colored paper squares.

    Outline in black pen.
    Tear around the outside of the pen line to give a ragged, rough line.

3. Paste the fruits and vegetables to look like they are tumbling out of the cornucopia.

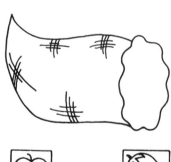

A Cornucopia Pull Out

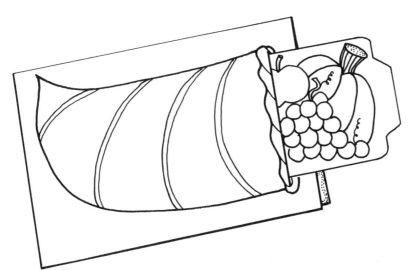

Your students will be delighted with this fall art project. It offers a movable surprise. Pull the tab and see the fall bounty. Push the tab back and it all disappears inside.

Materials:

- yellow construction paper
- reproducible pattern on page 42
- crayons and scissors

Steps to follow:

1. Fold the yellow paper in half.

   Cut a 5 1/2" (14.3 cm) slit in the top layer of the yellow paper. Make the slit 2" (5 cm) from the end.

2. Draw the cornucopia and color it brown.

   Add any details you like. Maybe mice peeking around, searching for lunch.

3. Cut out the pull tab on the dotted line.
   Fill this area with pictures of fall fruits and vegetables.

   Cut pictures from magazines or draw your own with crayons (see p. 42).

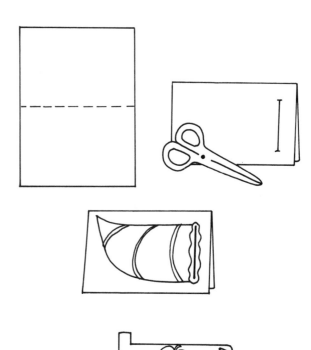

Seasonal Art

Pull Tab
for the
Cornucopia

pull

Drawing the Harvest

	1.	2.	3.	
pumpkin				Pumpkins may be *any* shape. Use the curved, vertical lines to create a feeling of roundness. The stem is also lined to show roundness.
acorn squash				Acorn squash have ridges.
crook-neck squash				Try drawing the "crook-neck" facing in different directions. Don't forget the little bumps.
grapes				Build your clump of grapes to any size you wish. Add a few tendrils curling among the grapes.
tangerine				Tangerines are flatter than oranges. Their dimples show more. They are also a deeper orange color.
walnuts				The walnut has a bumpy shell. A side view shows the two halves and the seam where the parts are joined.

Vegetable Prints

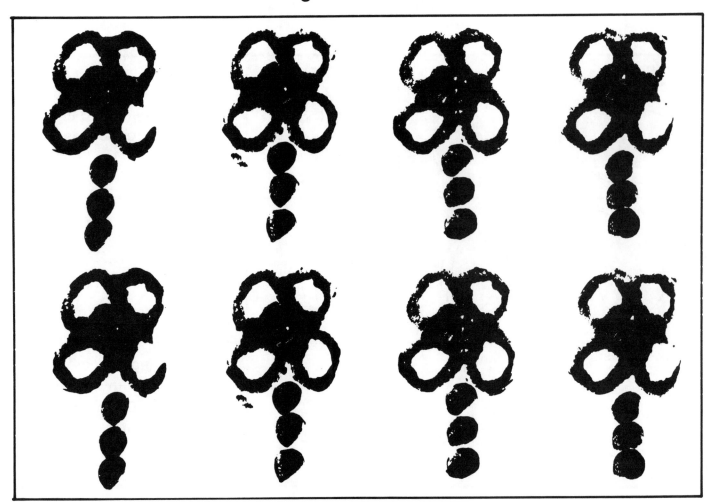

A trip to your local produce store is the first step in creating this colorful project. Be sure you have plenty of green peppers, zucchini, celery, and carrots. Onions are also effective.

Materials:
- vegetables cut in half
- tempera paint in flat dishes
- construction paper in various colors

Steps to follow:
1. Put small amounts of tempera in dishes.
2. Select a cut vegetable and dip in the paint. Place in position on construction paper.

The most successful prints make use of repetition of shapes and color. This is especially effective on borders.

Students may want to experiment on sheets of newsprint, saving construction paper for designs they want to keep.

Seasonal Art

Cross-Legged Pilgrim

Create a delightful Pilgrim boy to stand on your desk. Add a little imagination to the basic shape to create other characters of your own.

Materials:

- construction paper

  black -- 9" x 9" (22.8 cm x 22.8 cm) body

  3 " x 3" (7.5 cm x 7.5 cm) hat

  white -- 3" x 3" (7.5 cm x 7.5 cm) face

  1" x 3" (2.5 cm x 7.5 cm) hands and collar

  yellow -- 3" x 5" (7.5 cm x 13 cm) hair and buckles

- scissors, paste, crayons

- staplers

Steps to follow:

1. Fold the basic body piece.

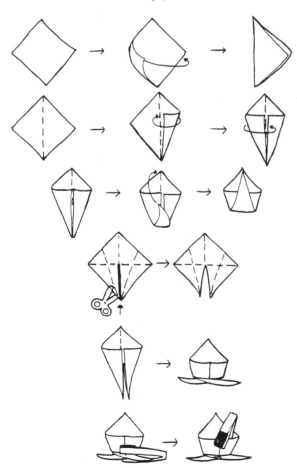

2. Cut out the other parts and paste to the basic body shape.

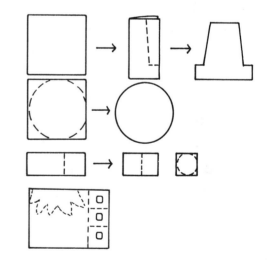

hat

face

collar
hands

hair
buckles

3. What will you put in Pilgrim's pocket?

Spelling words?

Popcorn?

Flowers?

Pilgrim Girl

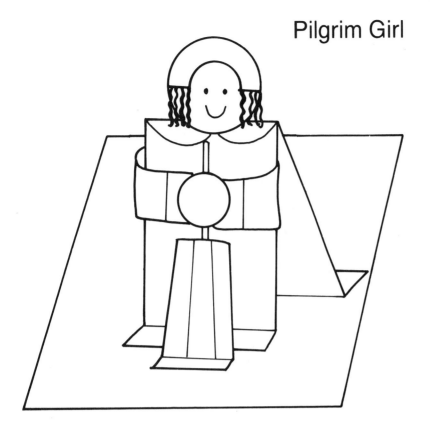

This three-dimensional Pilgrim girl is busy churning butter for the Thanksgiving feast. She can be made in any size appropriate to your grade level.

Materials:
- construction paper
  - gray—body, arms
  - white—head, collar, hands
  - green—background
  - brown—butter churn
- yarn—yellow, brown or black
- paste, scissors, crayons

Steps to follow:

1. Fold the main body piece.

   Paste the lower flaps to the green paper.

2. Wrap the arms around the front. Paste on the inside.

3. Cut the head from the white paper. Draw the cap and face with black crayon.

   Paste on yarn hair.

4. Cut out a butter churn.

   Paste in front of the girl and attach the churn handle to her arms.

5. Cut the collar and hands from the remaining white paper.

   Paste in place.

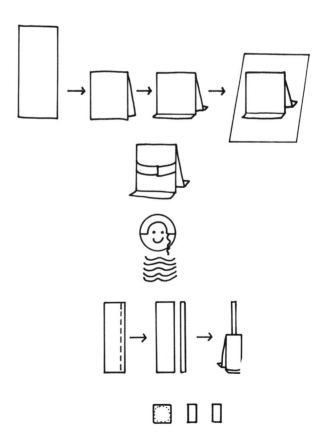

Indian Boy

This little brave has movable parts. He can sit on your arm or the edge of your desk.

Materials:
- construction paper
  brown 12" x 18" (30.5 cm x 45.7 cm)
     arms, body
  flesh -- 6" (15 cm) square for head
     3" (7.5 cm)
  black braids
- 2 paper-fasteners
- paste, scissors, crayons

Steps to follow:

1. Cut the arm strips off the brown body piece. Fold the remaining piece in half. Cut the leg slit and round the toes.

2. Round the corners of the head. Use crayons to color the hair, headband, and facial features. Paste the head to the body.

3. Round the tops of the arm strips. Cut two flesh-colored circles for hands. Paste to the arms.

   Attach the arms to the body with paper-fasteners.

4. Make "chain braids" and paste to each side of the head.

5. Use black crayon to draw fringe on the sleeves, legs and shirt.

6. Bend the Indian's legs and set him on your desk to explain "his version" of the First Thanksgiving.

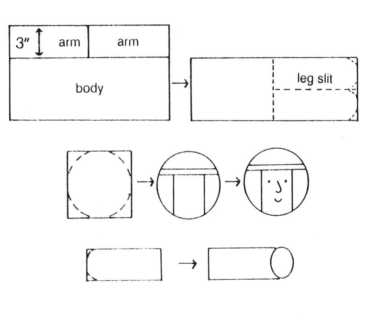

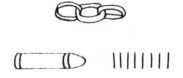

An Outstanding Turkey

This turkey has a spacer that holds the body and head away from the background paper to give it a real 3—D quality.

Materials:
- construction paper
    - background—any color
    - brown—body, wing, head, spacers
    - assorted colors for feathers
- straws for feet
- 2 beans for eyes
- scissors, paste, crayons

Steps to follow:

1. Round corners to create the body, head and wings.

2. Cut two strips of brown to use as spacers. Fold them.

   Paste one end to the turkey body and the other to the background paper. Follow the same process in attaching the head to the body. This guarantees the 3—D look.

3. Paste the wings on each side of the body.

4. Use paper scraps to create a beak and waddle. Glue on the two beans for eyes.

5. Cut and curl the feather strips and paste around the body. (See the picture.)

6. Paste on short strips of drinking straws for legs and feet.

7. Add a background with crayon. Maybe corn for the turkey to eat?

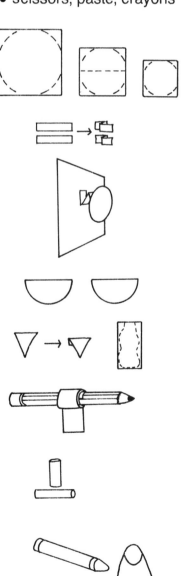

A Thanksgiving Mural

Would you like to recreate the first Thanksgiving celebration on your bulletin board? Here are some ideas to help get you started. The checklist and sign-up sheet on the following page is a good planning guide. Students sign for the contribution they wish to make.

Create the background sky and earth with paint, chalk or cut butcher paper. The scene can be created in a variety of ways:

> Paint or draw directly on the background.
> Paint or draw on other paper; then cut out and paste to the background.
> Cut pieces from construction paper and paste to the background for a collage effect.

Some research spent in the library will result in a more authentic scene.

   Seasonal Art

Mural Checklist

Select the item or person you want to make.
Sign your name by your choice.

Pilgrim Woman _____

Pilgrim Man _____

Pilgrim Girl _____

Pilgrim Boy _____

Chief Massasoit _____

Squanto _____

Indian Brave _____

Pilgrim houses _____

Wooden table and benches _____

Outdoor cooking fire _____

Baskets of corn _____

Baskets of pumpkins _____

Baskets of nuts _____

Cooked food for the table _____

Wild turkey _____

Deer _____

The forest background _____

Other _____

Winter

Snowball Chain

Each of these fellows is dressed uniquely for winter. The snowballs are what tie them all together.

Materials:
- Reproduce the pattern below.
- Construction paper cut in 4¼″ x 22″ strip (11.3 cm x 56 cm)

- Scissors and crayons

Steps to follow:

1. Fold your paper back and forth to match the width of the pattern 2 1/2" (6.3 cm).

2. Lay the pattern on the top of the folded paper and cut on the dotted lines.

3. Open your chain and use crayons to creatively dress each paper doll in its own wonderful winter wear.

4. Outline the snowball with black crayon. To make them really stand out, put a ring of glue around the snowball and sprinkle with glitter.

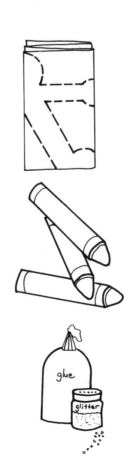

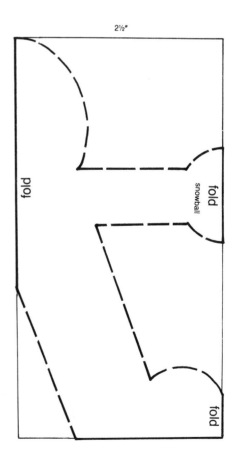

2½″

fold

fold
snowball

fold

53   Seasonal Art

A Hibernating Bear
Where did he go?

Here is a quick and easy way to enliven a class study of animal winter habitats.

Materials:
- White construction paper
  - 9" x 12" (22.8 cm x 30.5 cm)
- Crayons, pencil

Steps to follow:

1. Begin by folding the white construction paper.

2. Sketch in details in pencil first. Then add color.
   Draw the hill and entrance to the den (or burrow) on the top portion of your folded paper. Open the paper and draw the sleeping bear (or other hibernating animal) inside.

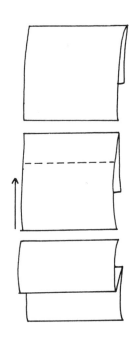

Seasonal Art

Snowman

Create this snowman with white sponge painting on blue construction paper. He will really sparkle if you sprinkle a small amount of silver glitter on the wet paint.

(or use salt paint)

Steps to follow:

1. Sponge paint the snowman shape. *Alternate - tear 3 paper circles lg, med, sm.*

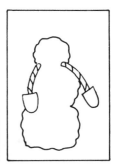

2. Poke two holes to thread yarn through. Cut mittens from folded construction paper and glue to the ends of the yarn.

3. Use construction paper scraps or found objects (buttons, cloth, beans, beads, popcorn) to create a face, hat and buttons for the snowman.

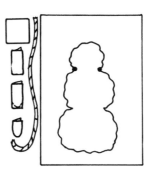

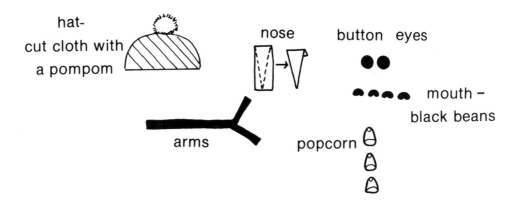

hat-
cut cloth with a pompom

nose

button eyes

arms

mouth –
black beans

popcorn

Penguins Sliding to the Sea

Watch these penguins slide down the ice floe. Children enjoy the three-dimensional effect.

Materials:
- White construction paper
  9" x 12" (22.8 cm x 30.5 cm) background
  2" x 3 1/2" (5 cm x 8.8 cm) penguin bodies
- Orange scraps for beaks
- Black scraps for wings
- Blue tissue strips
  2" x 9" (5 cm x 22.8 cm)
- Crayons, paste, scissors
- Liquid starch

Steps to follow:

1. Use a black crayon to outline the ice floe. (Older students can brush the paper with liquid starch and lay one sheet of pale blue tissue over the whole page to represent an ice floe. Let dry, then draw with black crayon.)

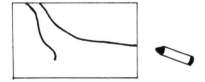

2. Cut wave lines on top edge of tissue strips. Adhere one or two strips of tissue with brushed-on liquid starch. Allow the blue tint to smear up onto the snow slide. Let the background dry.

3. Prepare the penguins by rounding off the top corners of the white rectangles. Fold up the edge approximately 1/2" (1.3). Draw the basic penguin design on your rounded shape.

Cut out an orange scrap for a beak. Fold the back edge. Paste that edge to the penguin.
Cut two small black rectangles for wings. Round one end of each wing. Paste wings to your bird.

4. Paste the lower edge of the penguins to the ice floe.

Seasonal Art

Positive-Negative Trees

Experimenting with different tree shapes helps widen your students' awareness of the variations in nature.
Developing a positive-negative design is fun and the contrast is striking.

Materials:
- Construction paper
  White 12" x 18" (30.5 xm 45.7 cm) background
  Blue 6" x 18" (15 cm x 45.7 cm) sky
- Scissors, pencil, and paste

Steps to follow:
Before beginning, display a wide variety of tree outline shapes on the chalkboard.

1. Lay the blue paper on the top half of the white paper.

    Sketch a line of tree shapes with your pencil. The base of the tree must come to the lower edge of the blue paper. You may use all one shape or many variations. Trees don't need to be the same height.

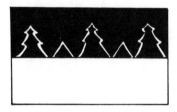

2. Cut out the trees following your pencil line.

3. Paste the blue sky paper to the top half of your white background paper (WITHOUT the cut-out trees).

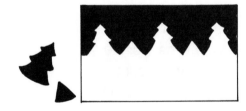

    Now lay the trees back in their original spots. Put paste on the backs (one tree at a time) and carefully flip the tree down to form a shadow for the white tree. Be sure the base lines line up. Paste the rest of the tree shadows down.

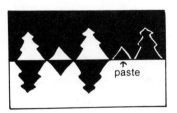

paste

Seasonal Art

Animal Tracks
Who made them?

Use your school library as a resource for discovering types of animal tracks. Encyclopedias usually have a whole section devoted to this topic. You may use this activity as a motivation for writing exciting stories about what the tracker is about to discover.

Materials:
- White construction paper
    12" x 18" (30.5 cm x 45.7 cm)
        background
    4" x 4" (10 cm x 10 cm) flap
- Crayons, pencils with erasers
- Paste
- Black tempera plus fingers

Steps to follow:

1. Fold down a 1/2" (1.3 cm) flap on the 4" x 4" (10 cm x 10 cm) paper. Paste this flap to the background sheet. Think about what animals have left tracks in the snow.

2. Use crayon to draw the bare winter trees. Draw a black horizon line. Draw the entrance to a cave on the flap. Color it.

3. Lift the cave flap. Draw an animal underneath.

4. Now use your fingers or the eraser on a pencil to print rows of tracks on your paper. Dip your fingers (or pencil eraser) into the black paint and then print on the paper. Remember what you learned about tracks in your encyclopedia.
   Invent a story about what happened to all the creatures that made these tracks.

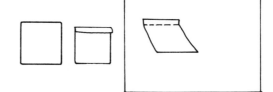

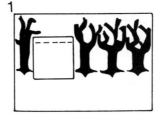

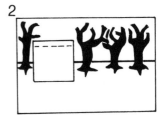

Polar Bear and Eskimo Puppets

Put the Eskimo on one hand and the polar bear on the other. Now you're ready to share what you've learned about their homeland. Or you might want to create an adventure for the two characters to act out.

Materials:
• Reproduce the patterns on pages 60-61
• Crayons, scissors and glue

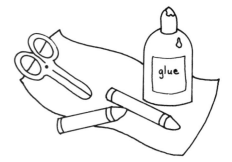

Steps to follow:

1. Eskimo
   Color the Eskimo and cut out the pattern.
   Fold on the center line and paste around the edges.
   Slip a hand inside the puppet.

2. Polar Bear
   Color the bear pattern. Cut out the back and the front of the pattern. Apply paste around the side and top of the pieces. Paste the front to the back. Tell a story with the puppet.

 Seasonal Art

Eskimo Puppet Pattern

Seasonal Art

Polar Bear

back

front

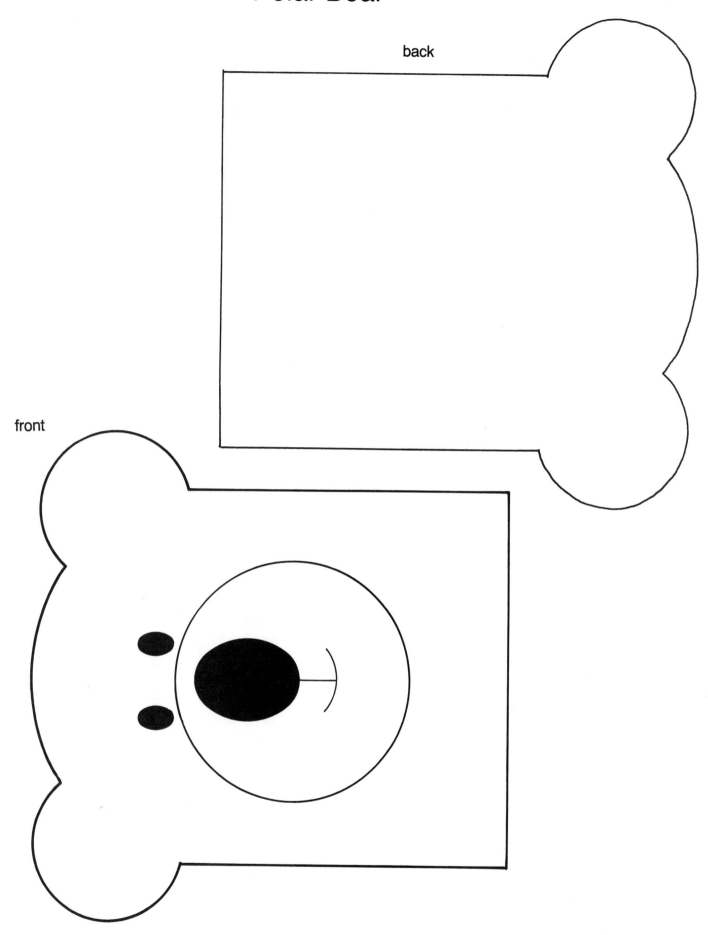

Seasonal Art

Toboggan Kids

This art lesson can be used on a bulletin board with great success or to add interest to creative stories about winter fun.

Materials:
- Reproduce the pattern on the following page on white construction paper.
- Brown construction paper 8 1/2" x 3 1/2" (21.8 cm x 8.8 cm) toboggan
- Crayons
- Scissors
- Paste

Steps to follow:

1. Color all pattern pieces.
   Draw faces.
   Design sweaters or jackets.
   Add designs to scarves and caps

2. Cut out all pieces. Paste a hat and scarf to each person.

3. Curl end of toboggan. (A pencil is good for this.)

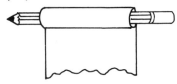

4. Fold the bottom piece of each child under. Fold the arms up. Paste the hands of the front kid to the toboggan. Paste the hands of the back kid to the back of the front kid.

Bulletin board:

Cover the board with blue paper. Attach strips of white butcher paper loosely to the board to form toboggan runs. Tape or glue toboggans to the snow runs.

Pattern for Toboggan Kids

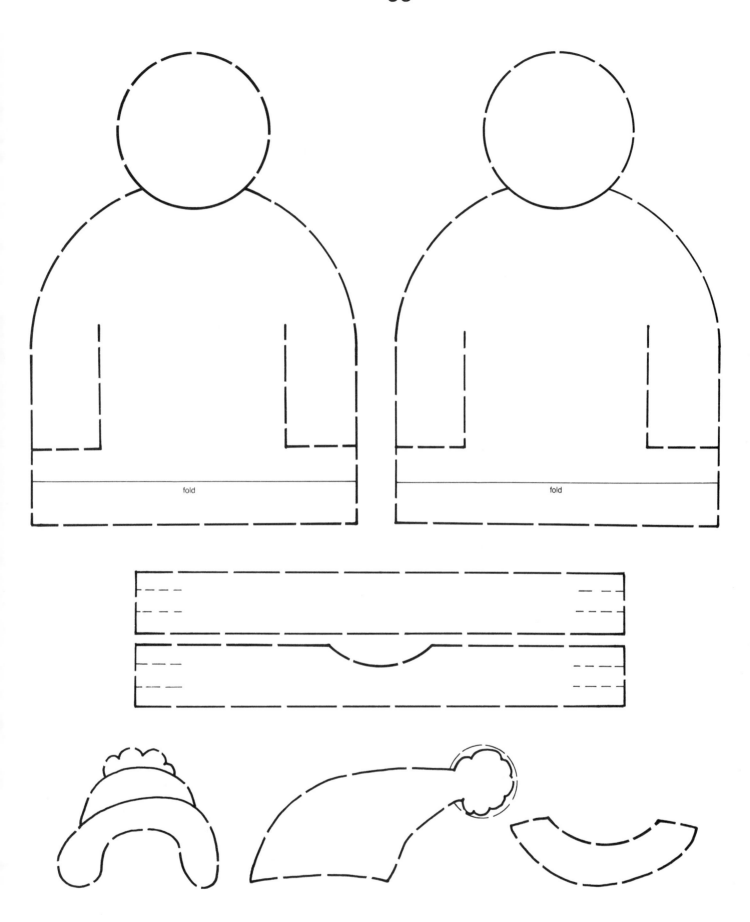

fold

fold

Snowflake Mobiles

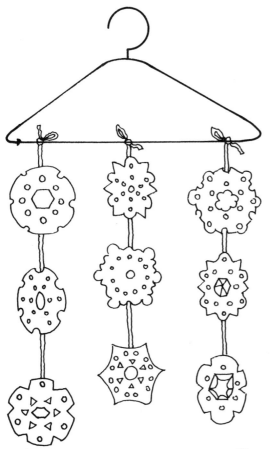

Bring the beauty of a winter snowfall indoors. Hang lacy snowflakes in your windows or from your ceiling and enjoy their movement.

Materials:
- Hangers
- Yarn
- White paper squares
- Use lightweight paper for ease in cutting
- 4" x 4" (10 cm x 10 cm) squares are a good size
- Scissors
- Hole punch

Steps to follow:

1. Round off the corners to create a circle.

2. Fold the circle.

3. Create your design with scissors and/or a hole punch. Open the finished snowflake.

4. Paste several snowflakes to a length of yarn. Tie yarn to a clothes hanger.

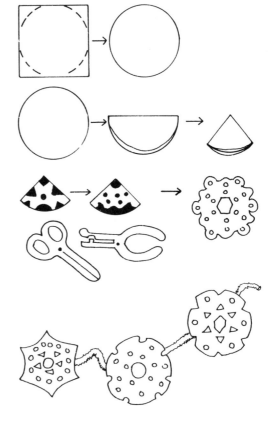

Seasonal Art

Christmas Design Fun

This project offers the excitement of experimenting with contrasting colors and interesting shapes to create pleasing designs. A small version may be used as a greeting card. Larger forms may be displayed in a quilt-like design on a bulletin board. Colors and shapes can be selected to fit a specific season or holiday.

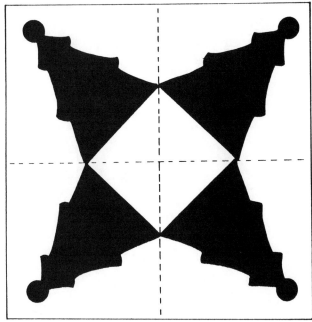

Materials:
- White construction paper
  12" x 12" (30.5 cm x 30.5 cm)
- Templates in various designs cut
  from 6" (15 cm) squares
- Green Construction paper cut 1/4
  the size of the white 6" x 6" (15 cm x 15 cm)
- Red paper scraps
- Scissors, paste, pencil, crayon

Steps to follow:

1. Create templates out of tagboard. Use simple shapes appropriate to the season.
2. Chose one template. Trace around it on four green squares. Cut out on the trace lines.
3. Fold the white paper into quarters.
4. Arrange the green shapes around the center of the white paper. Place one shape in each quarter section. Paste in place.
5. Cut small design shapes from red paper and add to the design.
   Use crayons to add final details.

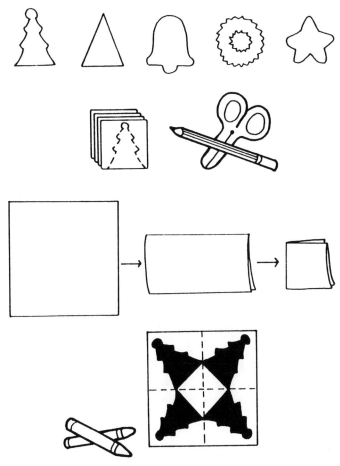

Seasonal Art

Stencil Your Own Wrapping Paper

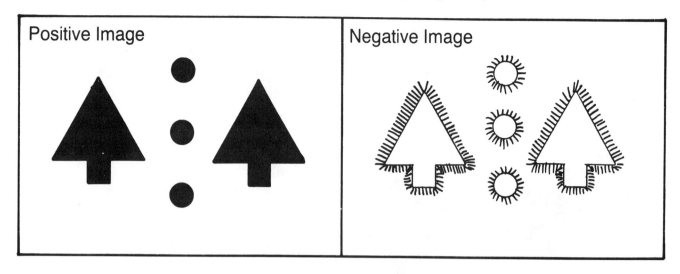

| Positive Image | Negative Image |

Practice design skills as you learn how to use stencil techniques in creating your own wrapping paper. This activity stresses:

1. development (by teacher and/or students) of a workable stencil pattern.
2. planning a pleasing design.
3. learning that each stencil pattern has a negative and positive image.

Materials:
- Tag squares 4" x 4" (10 cm x 10 cm) for cutting stencils
- Exacto knife, scissors
- Paint, crayons or colored pencils
- Paint brushes, sponges, or toothbrushes
- Large sheets of newsprint

use mural paper & tape to the wall!

Steps to follow:
1. Cut a stencil design. Something simple works best. Save both parts.
2. Select the medium you wish to use: paint, crayons, pencils.
3. Creating a positive image: Use the tag square. Place the stencil on your paper and fill in the empty area with color. (If you use paint, lift the stencil carefully to avoid smears.) Place the stencil in a new position. Repeat until the design is complete.
4. Creating a negative image: Use the cut-out pattern. Using crayon, pencil or paint (a toothbrush works well), brush color out from the edges of the stencil. Lift the stencil and place in a new position. Repeat until the design is complete.
5. You may also try combining the negative and positive images to create an interesting design.

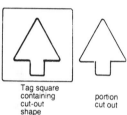

Tag square containing cut-out shape

portion cut out

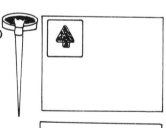

Seasonal Art

Lace A Stocking

Steps to follow:

1. Cut out the two stockings (for front and back).
2. Plan your design. Then decorate the stocking.

   What can you do?

Cut Paper	Paint	Crayon
stripes	sponge	create red
dots	& paint	and green
your name	finger–	designs
zigzags	paints	
	water	
	colors	

Create the same design on the front and back of the stocking.

3. Punch holes around the stockings about 1″ apart. (Do both stockings at the same time, so the holes will line up for lacing.)
4. Lace the front and back pieces together. Pull the yarn through the needle and begin at the top of the stocking. Tie a knot around the first hole. Now lace around the stocking. Tie a knot at the end.
5. Hang your stocking up to be admired.

Your students can produce colorful Christmas stockings while they practice their coordination skills. Finished stockings can be stuffed with a "surprise" or used to hold Christmas stories or messages.

Materials:
- Reproduce the stocking pattern on card stock or construction paper (two per child).
- Needle
- Paper scraps, paint , or crayons
- Yarn (36″ per stocking) (91.5 cm)
- Scissors and paste
- Hole punch

Seasonal Art

Reindeer Card Holder

This project makes a lovely Christmas present to send home for Mom. It is a colorful way to collect all those Christmas cards that arrive in the mail.

Materials:
- Red butcher paper
- Construction paper
  - brown   7" x 12" (18 cm x 30.5 cm) body
  -            5" x 3" (13 cm x 7.5 cm) ears
  - brown   6" x 8" (15 cm x 20.5 cm) antlers and eyes
  - green   7" x 3" (18 cm x 7.5 cm) halter
  - red   2 1/2" x 2 1/2" (6.3 cm x 6.3 cm) nose
- Yarn (optional)
- Scissors, paste, stapler
- Hanger

Steps to follow:

1. Staple the red butcher paper to the hanger.
2. Fold up the bottom three times in 4" (10 cm) segments. Staple the edges to create a pocket.
3. Cut out the reindeer pieces and paste to the butcher paper so the reindeer's head is just below the hanger hook.

   Use the black paper scraps to cut out eyes.

   The nose can be extra special if you...
   a. put a spacer behind the red circle to make it stand out.
   b. cut the red circle larger. Cut in and overlap to make a cone-shaped nose.
   c. make a red yarn pompom that's fun to rub.

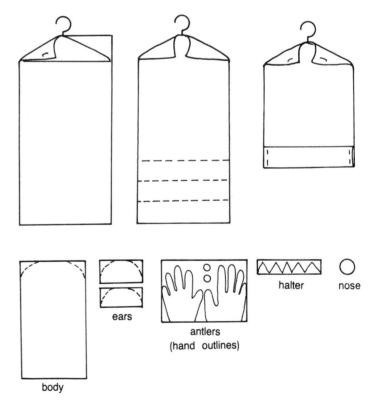

body

ears

antlers
(hand outlines)

halter

nose

Christmas Banners

words only

words and pictures

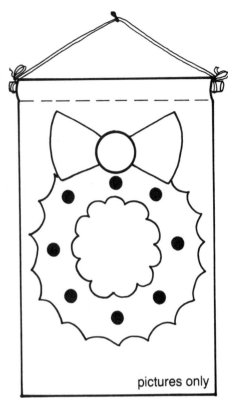

pictures only

Hang these cheerful banners in windows, on doors, or on your front porch to wish a merry time to family and friends.

Materials:
• Butcher paper
  18" x 36" (45.7 cm x 91.5 cm) narrow banner
  24" x 36" (61 cm x 91.5 cm) wide banner
• Doweling, bamboo plant support, twig... to hold banner
• Construction paper in assorted colors
• Paste or glue
• Scissors
• Yarn
• Letter templates

Steps to follow:

Spend some time discussing possible designs, words to use, appropriate pictures, and techniques for tracing and cutting letters or how to create "fat" letters using marking pens. Children may choose to make a preliminary sketch on scratch paper before beginning finished project.

1. Fold both ends of butcher paper over twice (about 2" (5 cm) folds). Paste or staple bottom fold.
2. Cut out pieces for banner from construction paper. Arrange entire design on butcher paper. When satisfied with the look, paste the pieces down.
3. Attach doweling to top of banner with paste or staples. Add yarn and hang.

Seasonal Art

Sleigh and Reindeer

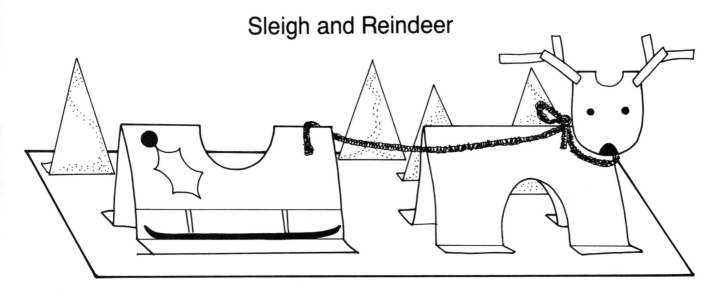

Create a delightful three-dimensional scene to display for Christmas.

Materials:
- Construction paper
  - white 9" x 12" (22.8 cm x 30.5 cm)
  - red 7" x 4" (18 cm x 10 cm)
  - brown 6" x 3 1/2" (15 cm x 8.8 cm)
- Scissors, paste
- Crayon, pencil, yarn

Steps to follow:

1. Sleigh
   a. Fold the red paper in half. Cut out a half circle on the fold.
      Fold up the two bottom edges.
   b. Sketch the sleigh with your pencil on front and back sides. Outline the sleigh and runners with black crayon. Why not decorate the sleigh with some green holly?

2. Reindeer
   a. Fold the brown paper in half. Cut out a half circle from the open sides. Save the ⌂ for the reindeer's head. Fold up the bottom of the reindeer's feet.
   b. Paste one of the cut out ⌂ to the body. Cut out a small curve from the top to form ears. Use the remaining brown scrap to create antlers. Paste to the reindeer's head.
      Use crayons to add facial features.

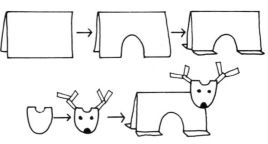

3. Paste the bottom folds of the sleigh and reindeer to the white background paper.
   Tie a loop of yarn around the reindeer's neck. Attach the other end to the sleigh.

4. You may want to add green pine trees.

Rudolph Pop-Up Card

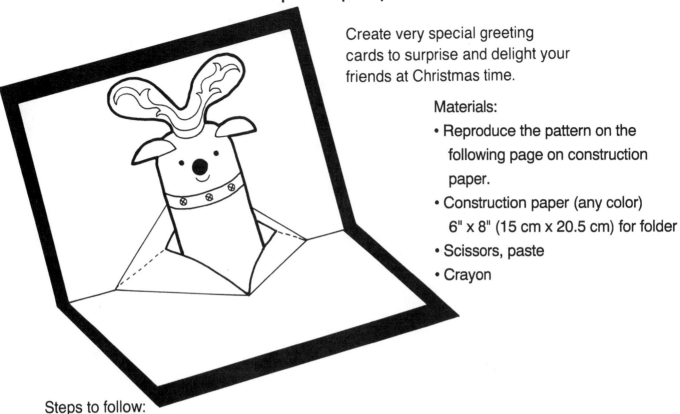

Create very special greeting cards to surprise and delight your friends at Christmas time.

Materials:
- Reproduce the pattern on the following page on construction paper.
- Construction paper (any color) 6" x 8" (15 cm x 20.5 cm) for folder
- Scissors, paste
- Crayon

Steps to follow:

1. Color reindeer brown with a red nose.

2. Cut out reindeer pieces. Paste ears and antlers to reindeer's head.

3. Prepare pop-up patterns. Form A:
   a. Cut out the basic form.
   b. Fold in half. Cut on dotted lines.
   c. Fold back the
   d. Open the paper and push the tab to the reverse side.

   Form B:
   a. Cut out the form.
   b. Cut on dotted line.
   c. Fold on fold lines.
   d. Open and reverse folds by pushing them inside.

4. Putting card together:

   a. Fold construction paper in half to create outside folder.
   b. Put paste around outside edges of Form A. Paste inside folder. Be sure the folder edges meet securely.
   c. Put paste around outside edges of Form B. Paste inside folder, over Form A. Be sure the folded edges meet securely.
   d. Put paste on the tab front. Attach reindeer to the tab. Be sure the bottom of the reindeer touches the fold line.

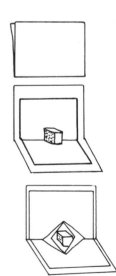

Seasonal Art

Pattern for the Rudolph Pop-up Card

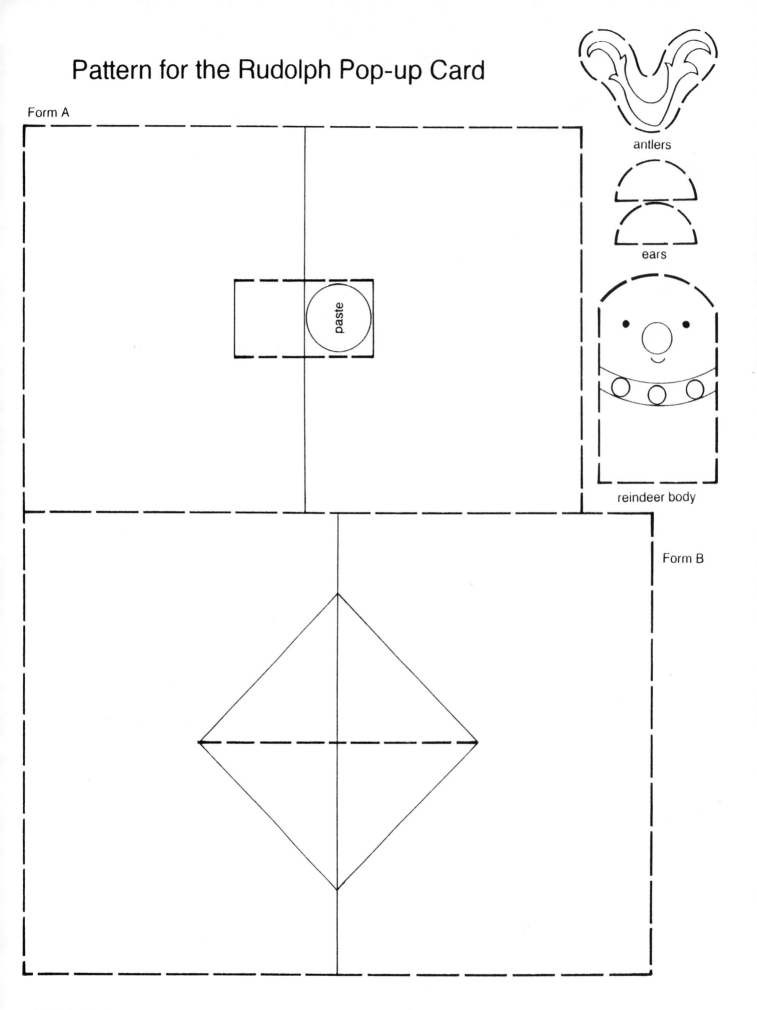

Form A

antlers

ears

paste

reindeer body

Form B

Seasonal Art

Cross-Legged Elf

Create a delightful little elf to stand on your desk. Add a little imagination to the basic shape to create other characters of your own.

Materials:
- Construction paper
  - green/red   9" x 9" (22.8 cm x 22.8 cm) body
  -                3" x 3" (7.5 cm x 7.5 cm) hat
  - white   3" x 3" (7.5 cm x 7.5 cm) face
  -            1" x 3" (2.5 cm x 7.5 cm) hands and collar
  - black   1" x 3" (2.5 cm x 7.5 cm) hair
- Scissors, paste, crayons
- Stapler

Steps to follow:

1. Fold the basic body piece.

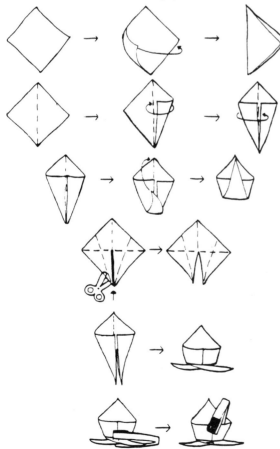

2. Cut out the other parts and paste to the basic body shape.

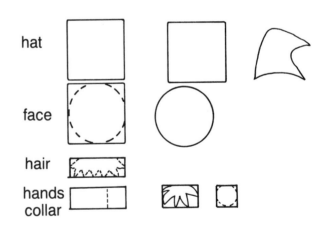

hat

face

hair

hands collar

Curl the elf's toes.

3. What will you put in the elf's pocket?
   Spelling words?
   A snack?
   Christmas wishes?

Seasonal Art

Draw an Elf or a Toy Soldier

These basic drawing suggestions are just a beginning. Allow students time to improvise, change and develop their own Christmas characters after you have drawn together and established the basic steps with everyone. Eliminate the phrase— "I don't know how to draw it!"

An elf

A toy soldier

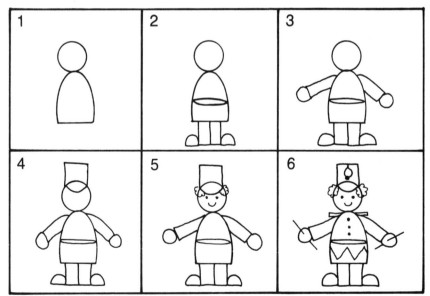

Now draw the elf and toy soldier again. This time try to make it appear that its knees are bent or that its arms are held up.

Why not risk it all and see if you can draw a side view of these characters. You can begin with the very same basic shapes.

Seasonal Art

A Christmas Angel

(to hang on your tree)

Reproduce the angel pattern on page 76 . Add your special touches to make her sparkle on your tree.

Steps to follow:

1. Color the angel and her candle.
2. Cut on the heavy dotted lines. Fold on the light dotted lines.
3. Add a line of glue and glitter to the lower edge. Lick and stick stars can also make a nice border.

4. Draw a face on the angel's head. Put a glitter halo in her hair. Glue the head to the body.

5. Punch a hole through the top of the wings and thread a strip of yarn through. Tie a loop. The yarn will hold the angel together and allow you to hang it on the tree.

       Seasonal Art

Christmas Angel Pattern

paste

Seasonal Art

Santa Paper Doll

Dress this Santa for any occasion. What would he wear to a swimming party, to an Easter egg hunt, or to the zoo? What does he wear when he and Mrs. Santa work in the garden? Is red his favorite color or does he just prefer it in the winter?

Reproduce the Santa paper doll pattern on page 78. Use construction paper or card stock. Children may color and cut it out. Now they are ready to create his wardrobe.

Steps to follow:

1. Tape the paper doll to a window.
2. Tape white paper over it so you can see the doll shape through the paper. Draw the piece of clothing to fit Santa.
3. Color the clothing and add tabs so the clothes will stay on the paper doll. Cut out the clothing.
4. Dress Santa in his new outfit and explain to a friend why you made that choice.

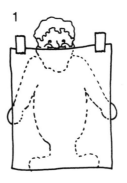
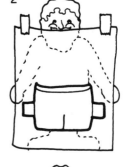

Seasonal Art

Santa Paper Doll Pattern

Seasonal Art

Draw Santa, His Reindeer, and His Sleigh

Follow the steps to create pictures of Santa, his reindeer, and his sleigh. Do the first drawings together, so that your students are comfortable with the basic forms. Encourage them to think of interesting backgrounds.

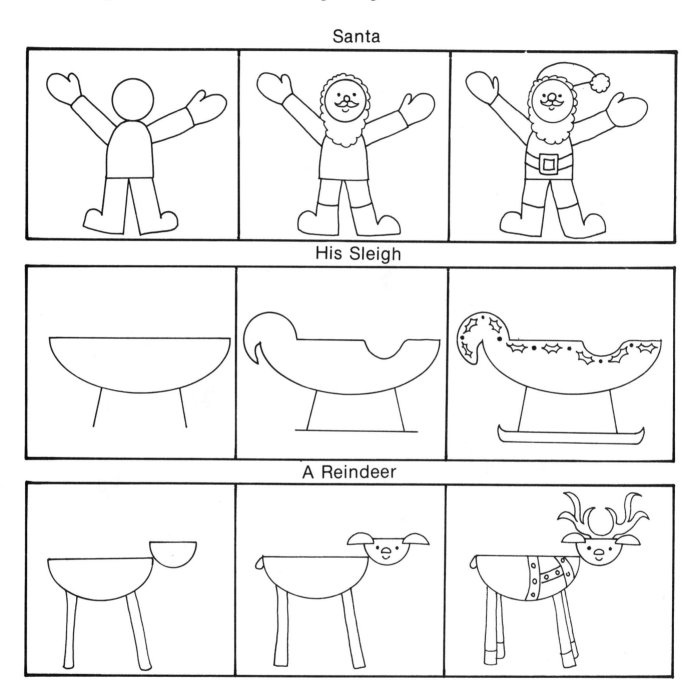

Santa

His Sleigh

A Reindeer

Now, let the children create their own pictures by placing the three drawings in interesting arrangements and using their imaginations to create an appropriate background.

Are there packages in the sleigh? Is the reindeer pulling the sleigh to the top of a house? Does Santa have his pack flung over his shoulder?

Encourage your students to make their pictures tell a story.

 Seasonal Art

Festive Thumb Prints

The materials needed for this activity are close at hand! Pull out a fresh stamp pad and get your fingers ready to press into service! Experiment with shapes and designs on newsprint before making a finished product.

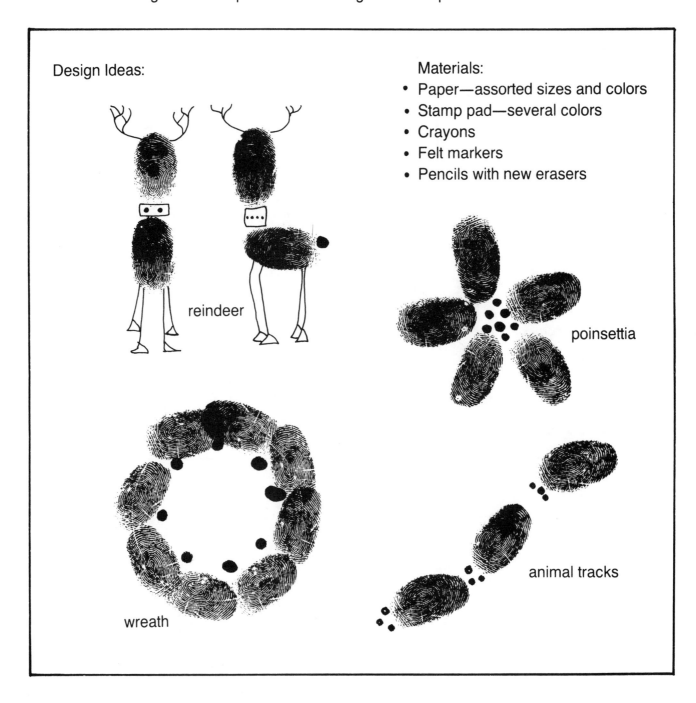

Design Ideas:

Materials:
- Paper—assorted sizes and colors
- Stamp pad—several colors
- Crayons
- Felt markers
- Pencils with new erasers

reindeer

poinsettia

wreath

animal tracks

These thumb print designs are clever Christmas card illustrations. They may also be used successfully as border designs for framing Christmas stories. Use colored stamp pads for festive results. Crayons or fine point felt markers can be used to add details. The rubber eraser on a pencil makes a useful stamp for eyes, berries, etc.

Seasonal Art

A Remarkable Candy Cane

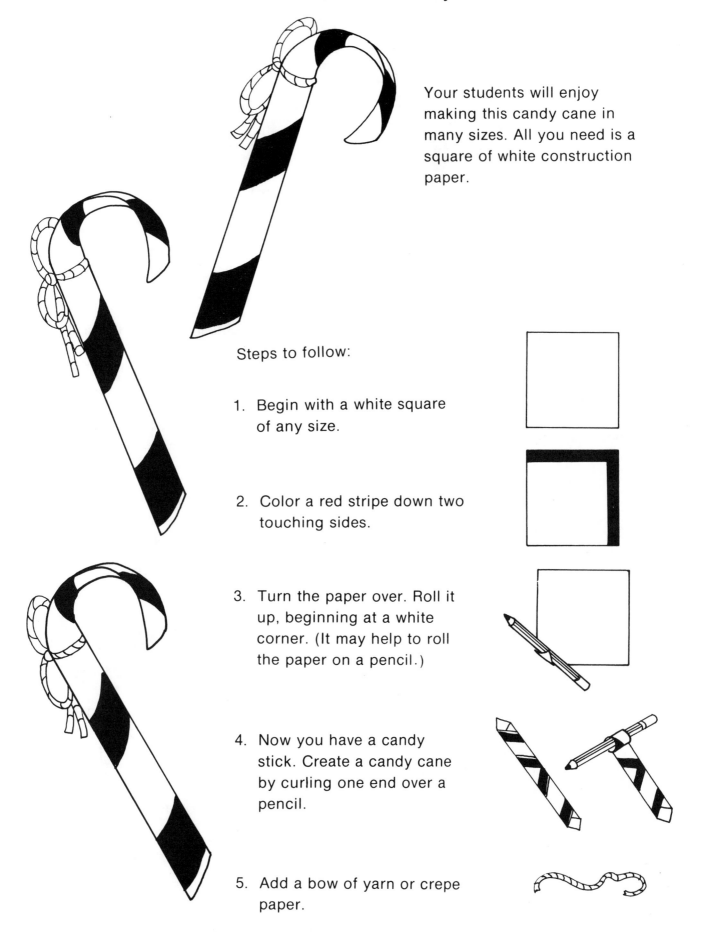

Your students will enjoy making this candy cane in many sizes. All you need is a square of white construction paper.

Steps to follow:

1. Begin with a white square of any size.

2. Color a red stripe down two touching sides.

3. Turn the paper over. Roll it up, beginning at a white corner. (It may help to roll the paper on a pencil.)

4. Now you have a candy stick. Create a candy cane by curling one end over a pencil.

5. Add a bow of yarn or crepe paper.

Seasonal Art

Light the Menorah

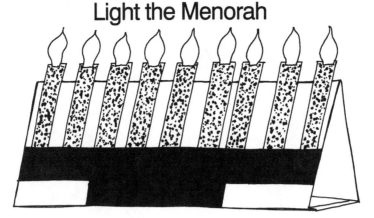

Hanukkah, or Chanukah, the Jewish Festival of Lights, celebrates the triumph of the Jews over their Syrian conquerors over 2000 years ago. Hanukkah is called the Festival of Lights because of the story surrounding the relighting of the oil lamp in the temple in Jerusalem.

There are nine candles, one for each of the eight days of Hanukkah, and a middle candle called the shammas, or servant candle. It is used to light the other candles.

Materials:
- construction paper
  - 1 - blue 12" x 18" (30.5cm x 45.7cm)
  - 9 - yellow 2" x 1" (5.0cm x 2.5cm)
  - 9 - white 4" x 1" (10.0cm x 2.5cm)
  - 1 - black 11" x 2" (28.1cm x 5.0cm)
  - 1 - black 6" x 1" (15.0cm x 2.5cm)

- paste, scissors, tape

Steps to follow:

1. Fold blue paper in half crossways, then fold a 2" base.

2. Build the menorah from the bottom up.
   a. Paste the smallest black piece near the bottom center of the blue background.

   b. Paste the larger black piece above the first.

   c. Paste the middle candle first. Then lay four candles on either side. Check spacing before pasting down.

   d. Fold the yellow pieces in half lengthwise, holding the fold and cutting "hill" to a point at one end. Paste to the end of candles for flames.

3. Fold blue paper to stand up. Tape base together.

Seasonal Art

Hanukkah Holiday Cards

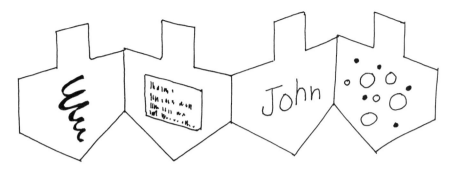

The basic fold shown below is the beginning for a greeting card for the Hanukkah holiday season.

Reproduce the dreidel pattern below on tag to create templates for students to use.

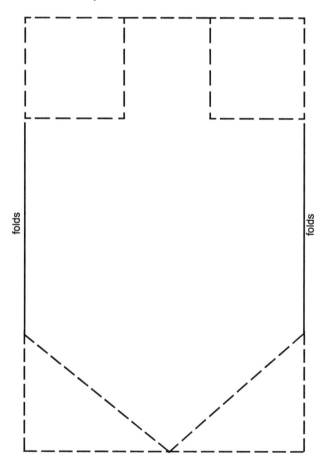

Reproduce this verse to paste to the dreidel card.

> Hanukkah,
> Eight special days.
> For sharing love
> In traditional ways.

Basic Fold:

Begin with a 4 1/2" x 12" (11.5cm x 30cm) sheet of construction paper.

Fold the paper in half.

Fold the top edge back to meet the fold.

Turn paper over and fold remaining edge back to fold.

Note: The edges of the folded paper must meet. You may want to do the folding for young children.

Steps to follow:

1. Trace pattern onto the top sheet of the folded card.

2. Cut out the dreidel shape. DO NOT cut through the sides.

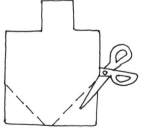

3. Paste the verse onto the second sheet. Children sign their name on the third sheet. Decorate the front and back sheets.

Seasonal Art

Dragon Headband
Wear it to celebrate Chinese New Year.

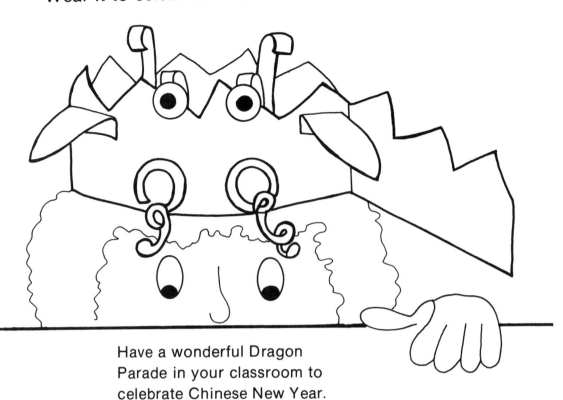

Have a wonderful Dragon Parade in your classroom to celebrate Chinese New Year. Everyone can wear this delightful dragon headband.

Steps to follow:

1. Cut a 12" x 18" (30.5 cm x 45.7 cm) sheet of green construction paper in zigzag cuts down the center of the paper.
2. Glue these pieces together to form the dragon.
3. Staple the headband to fit each student. Let the left-over hang down to become the dragon's tail.
4. Cut the rest of the dragon from colorful scraps of construction paper. Yellow, magenta and orange are good choices.

   Glue these pieces to the dragon.

   Enjoy your parade!

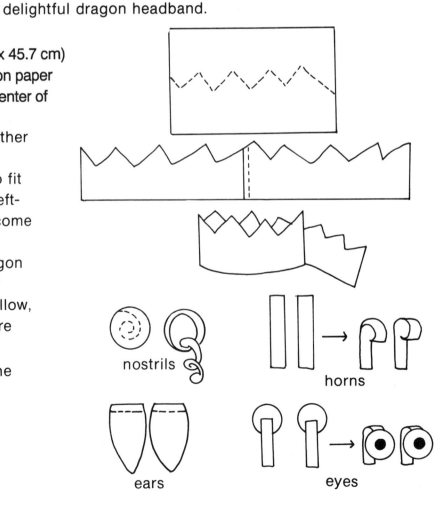

nostrils

horns

ears

eyes

Seasonal Art

Furnish Groundhog's Burrow

Set imagination to work to decorate the interior of groundhog's burrow. Start with an empty shoe box and see what develops.

Materials:
- Brown construction paper
  2" x 4" (5 cm x 10 cm) groundhog
  • Shoe or other small box
- Assorted odds and ends of paper and cloth
  wallpaper, wrapper paper, tinfoil, burlap, etc.
- Green tissue paper squares
  1" x 1" (2.5 cm x 2.5 cm)
- Glue, scissors, crayons, felt pens
- Exacto knife

Steps to follow:

1. Cut a 2 1/2" (6.3 cm) slit in one side of the box with the Exacto knife. (This becomes the top of the burrow.)

2. Make groundhog from the brown construction paper.

3. Color the top of the box with tissue paper "grass." Wrap tissue over pencil eraser, dip in glue and set on box.

4. Let students use their own imaginations to furnish groundhog's home.

   They might enjoy taking the project home to finish, then bringing it back to unveil the completed project.

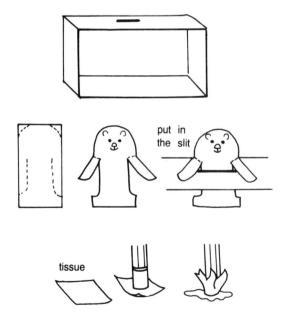

Groundhog Puppet

February 2 is Groundhog day.

What fun to watch groundhog peek out of his hole. Use the puppet to reinforce all the information you teach about the significance of Groundhog Day.

Materials:
- Reproduce the patterns on this and the following page.
- Tongue depressor
- Crayons, scissors, paste
- Stapler

Steps to follow:

1. Cut the dotted lines to create grass. Cut the slit on the fold line. Fold up on the line. Staple the sides.
Now color the sun yellow and the grass green.

2. Cut out the cloud. Decide if it will cover part of the sun or not. Paste it in place.

3. Color, then cut out the groundhog. Paste him to a tongue depressor. Slip the other end of the tongue depressor through the slit. Make sure the groundhog pops up and down.

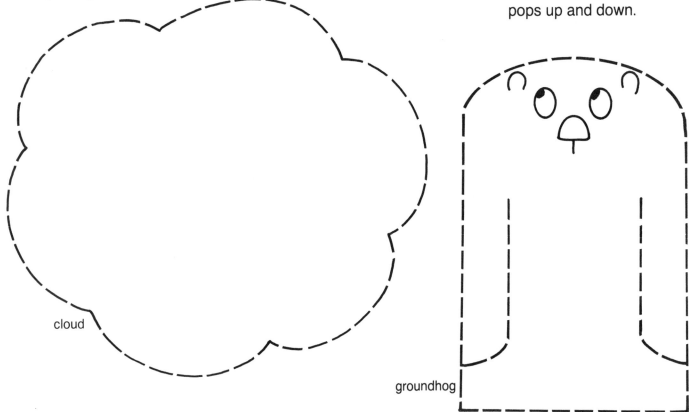

cloud

groundhog

Seasonal Art

February 2 is Groundhog Day.

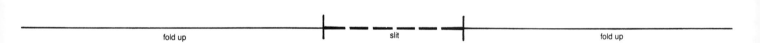

fold up   slit   fold up

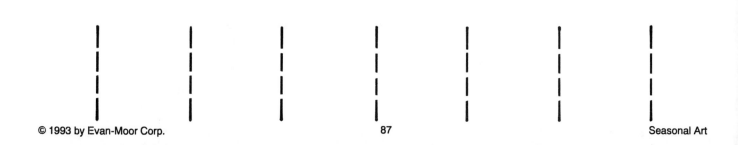

Seasonal Art

A Woven Valentine

Create a charming woven Valentine. It can be used for a greeting card, a basket for a small treat, or an ornament to hang on a tree.

Materials to use:
- Reproduce the pattern on the next page on white construction paper (OR on two shades of colored paper).
- Scissors
- Paste
- Crayons

Steps to follow:

1. Color the Valentine pieces; one section dark, one section light. Cut out on the dotted lines.
2. Fold over and weave each strip over and under.
3. Paste the loose edges down.

For a greeting card:
Open and write your message inside. Give to a special friend.

As a basket or ornament:
Paste the sides together, leaving the top open. Add a handle of construction paper.

Tuck a little treat or gift inside.

OR...
Make your basket in red and green to hang on your Christmas tree.

Seasonal Art

Pattern for a Woven Valentine

Run on construction paper.
Cut on dotted lines.

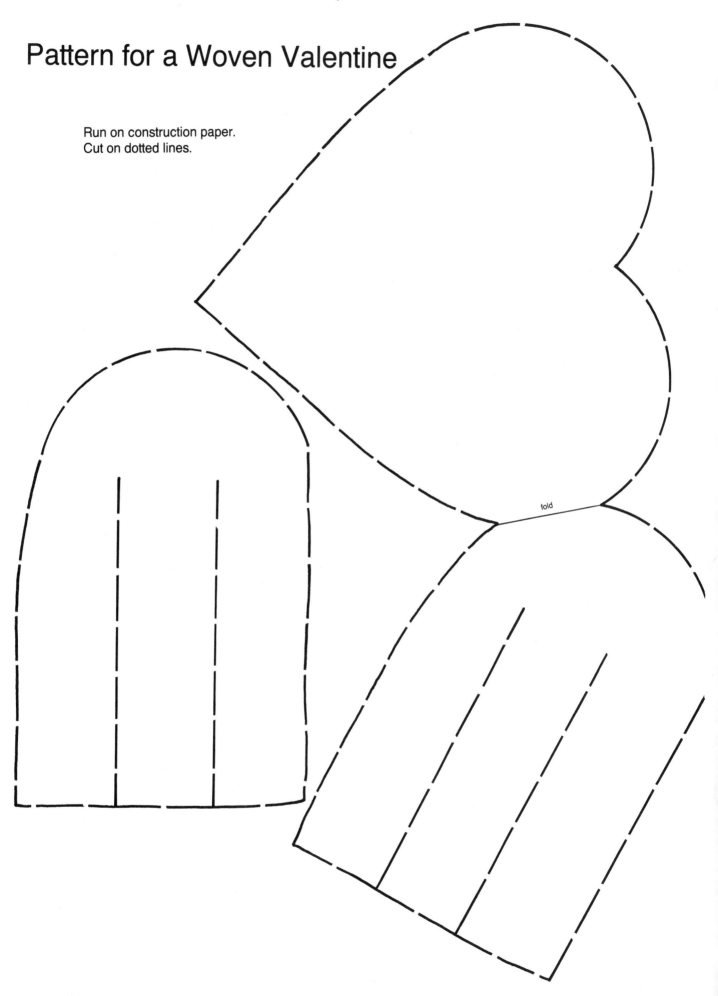

fold

Seasonal Art

Heart Baskets

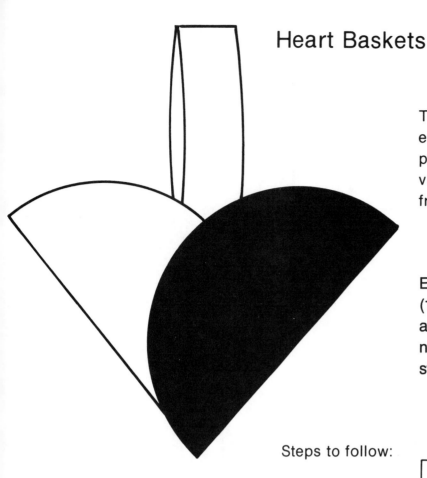

These delightful baskets are easy to create from construction paper. They will hold a small valentine treat for a special friend.

Each student will need two 4" (10 cm) squares, one red or pink and one white. They each will also need a 1" x 9" (2.5 cm x 22.8 cm) strip of red or pink for a handle.

Steps to follow:

1. Round off the corners of each square to form circles.

2. Fold each circle in half.

3. Put the two circles together as illustrated and paste the outside pieces together.

4. Paste the handle on the basket.

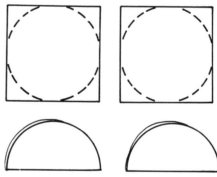

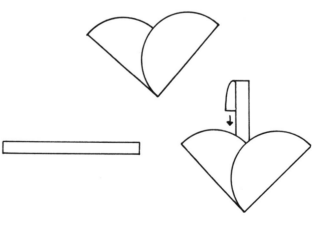

Note: You can use the same pattern to create Christmas ornaments. Make the circles from green and red squares.

Seasonal Art

Origami Valentine Pocket

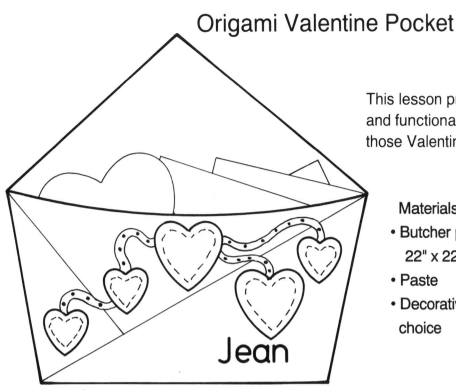

Jean

This lesson provides an attractive and functional way to pass out those Valentine cards in class.

Materials:
- Butcher paper, any color 22" x 22" (56 cm x 56 cm) square
- Paste
- Decorative supplies of your choice

Steps to follow:

1. Fold the butcher paper.

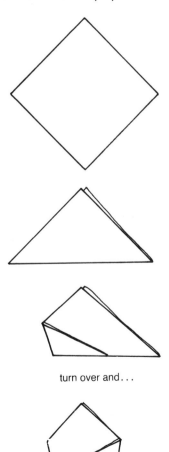

turn over and . . .

2. Tuck in the top flap between the folded sheets.
   Turn it over and tuck in the flap on the other side. (or leave it out to act as a closing flap which can be taped to the student's desk).

3. Decorate your Valentine pocket in your favorite style. They are striking when printed with heart-shaped sponges in bright colored paint. Glitter, doilies, ribbons and lace are always wonderful additions.
   The pockets can be pinned along a wall or to a bulletin board for easy distribution of Valentine cards.

Heart Chain Links

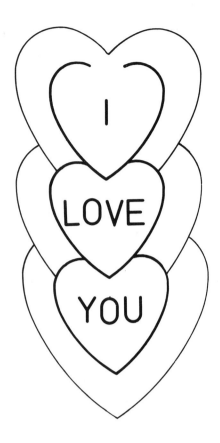

Long or short, this Valentine makes an exciting, versatile activity.

Materials:
• Construction paper square
  4" x 4" (10 cm x 10 cm)
  is a good size in various colors
• Scissors, felt pens, pencils

Steps to follow:

1. Fold the square in half. Hold on the fold and cut half a heart. (Younger students may need a pattern.)
   Cut a smaller heart on the inside, but stop before going all the way around.

2. Intertwine one heart with the next by slipping the heart point under the small inner heart of the next Valentine.

3. Now create a Valentine surprise.
   • Hang chains in the window.
   • Create a message by writing one letter on each heart. Disassemble and give to a friend.
   • Alternate colors (maybe each color in the rainbow).
   • Curl the center or decorate the edges.

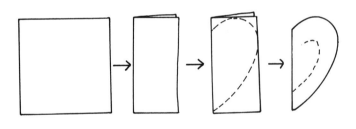

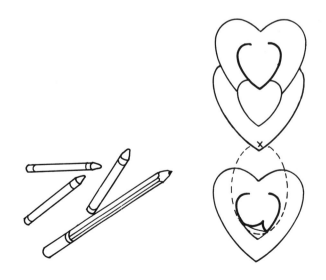

Pop-Up Valentines

What fun to receive a 3-dimensional Valentine greeting. Use this easy pop-up form to create a flock of special wishes for friends.

Materials:
- Reproduce the pattern on the following page.
- Construction paper 9" x 7" (22.8 cm x 18 cm) cover
- Paper scraps
- Paste, scissors
- Felt pens or crayons

Steps to follow:

1. Cut out your pattern page. Cut and fold the bird's beak.

2. Draw and color your Valentine bird.
   Add special touches with paper scraps.

3. Paste the bird into its cover. Put paste around edges only. Be sure the center folds touch exactly.

4. Write a Valentine message or poem on your card. Send it to a friend.

   Seasonal Art

Pop-Up Valentine Pattern

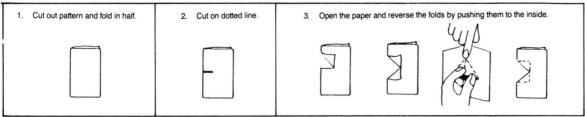

1. Cut out pattern and fold in half.
2. Cut on dotted line.
3. Open the paper and reverse the folds by pushing them to the inside.

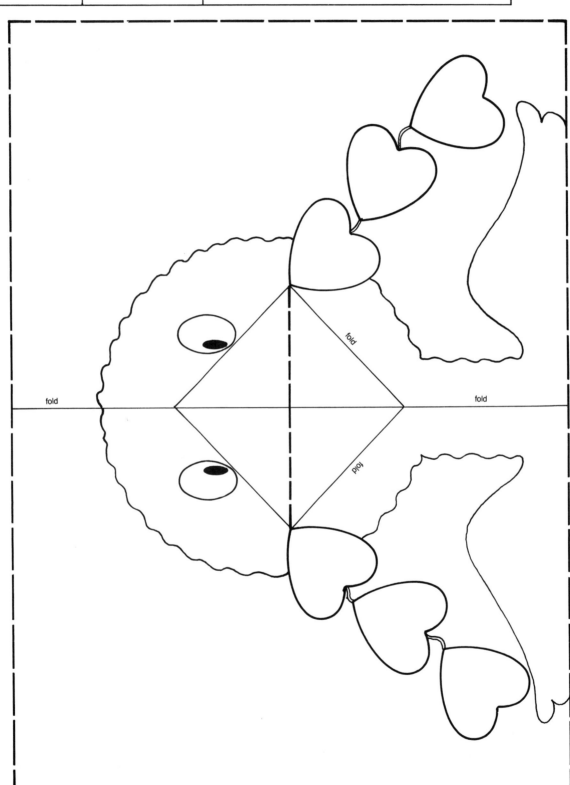

fold

fold

fold

fold

Seasonal Art

Valentine Mouse Book Mark

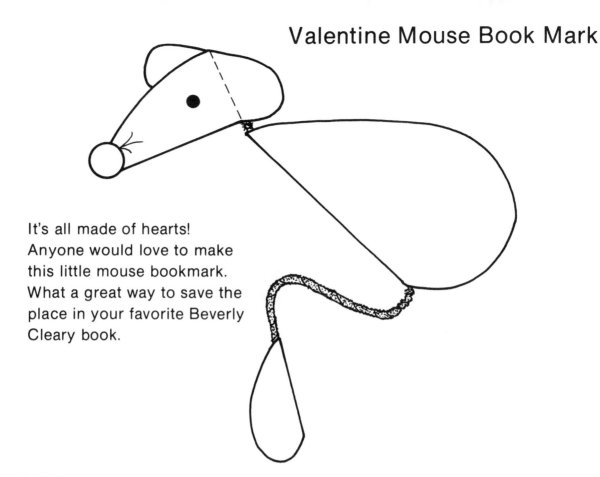

It's all made of hearts!
Anyone would love to make
this little mouse bookmark.
What a great way to save the
place in your favorite Beverly
Cleary book.

Steps to follow:

1. Begin with a 7" x 3" (18 cm x 7.5 cm)
   piece of white construction paper.

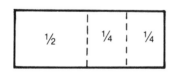

fold and cut

2. Cut hearts on the fold.

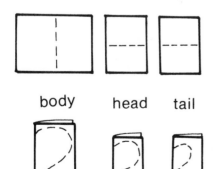

body   head   tail

3. Paste the yarn in the center
   of the hearts.

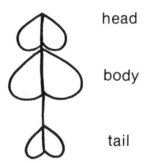

head

body

tail

Fold and paste the hearts shut.

4. Head:
   Add a pink circle for a
   nose, a black dot on both
   sides for eyes, and lines for
   little whiskers.
   Fold the round ears forward.

Seasonal Art

This activity provides exploration of the media of cut paper using the topic of hearts. Students are provided with an overview of techniques, then given time to explore the possibilities.

Materials:
- Newsprint
- Construction paper
    assorted sizes
    Valentine colors
- Scissors, pencil
- Hole punch

Steps to follow:

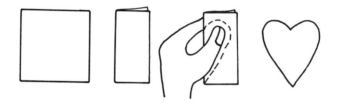

1. A heart needs to be symmetrical, so first teach students an easy way to cut a heart.
   Practice on newsprint until students perfect the process. Then use colored construction paper. Use squares approximately 4" x 4" (10 cm x 10 cm).

2. Experiment with making:
   - Tiny Valentines
   - Fat Valentines
   - Cut a heart within a heart
   - Cut and peel open the center
   - Punch holes in your heart
   - A broken heart (cut apart)
   - A heart with slits
   - A pleated heart

Save all these hearts and pin them up as a border for a February bulletin board or use them to create special Valentines for friends.

Seasonal Art

Heart Art—Part II

Put all the skill in designing hearts you accumulated in Part I of Heart Art into the creation of "heart-y" characters.

There are no steps to follow.
Here are some ideas to share with your students. They will generate many others with their own imaginations.

Materials:
- Construction paper assorted sizes and colors
- Lace doilies, ribbons, pipe cleaners, tinfoil, glitter, etc.
- Scissors, paste, crayons, felt pens
- Stapler, hole punch

Draw the Presidents

Follow these steps to create the perfect illustration for
your reports on Lincoln and Washington.

George Washington

Abraham Lincoln

 Seasonal Art

Abraham Lincoln's Log Cabin

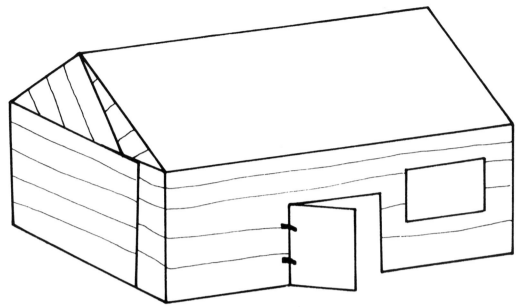

Materials:
- Brown construction paper
  9" x 12" (22.8 cm x 30.5 cm)
- Scissors
- Black crayon
- Paste

Made from one piece of construction paper, this free-standing log cabin is one you'll use again and again. Why not combine all of the students' cabins to create a whole village.

Steps to follow:

1. Fold paper into 16 boxes.
   (Fold in half 4 times.)

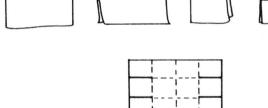

2. Open, then cut on the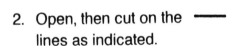
   lines as indicated.

3. Draw logs, door, and window.

   Cut door and fold open.
   Cut out window.

   Fold into a standing position
   by overlapping cut ends. Paste
   ends in place.

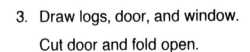

Spring

Spring Banner

Hang these lovely banners to bring a bit of spring into your classroom. They also provide the motivation for creative writing experiences.

Materials:
- Colored butcher paper
  24" x 12" (61 cm x 30.5 cm)
  (or non-glossy shelf paper)
- Water colors, brushes
- Black felt pen - fine point
- Yarn - 30" (76.5 cm)

Steps to follow:

1. Fold the top of your paper under twice. (about 1" (2.5 cm) each time.

2. Place yarn under the fold. Glue the fold down. Tie the yarn ends together.

3. Paint a spray of spring flowers down your banner, leaving room to write your spring verse.

4. Write a spring verse (couplet, haiku, cinquain) or copy a short spring poem you like. Use your best handwriting. Copy the poem with a black felt pen.

Seasonal Art

Raindrop Magic

Grab your slicker and enjoy the dripping weather outside! This is a great rainy day project.

Materials:
- White construction paper square 12" x 18" (30.5 cm x 45.7 cm)
- Crayons
- Dry blue tempera paint
- Flour sifter
- Raindrops (outside of course!)

Steps to follow:

1. Color a rainy day scene on white construction paper. Read *Rain* by Peter Spier as a source of inspiration. It is important crayon be applied evenly. Tell students not to color in the raindrops or to totally cover the sky area. Save that for later. The exciting part is coming soon.

2. Line students up against one wall with their coats on. The pictures should be on their desks. Walk around with a flour sifter full of dry blue tempera paint. Sift a thin layer of paint over the sky area of the picture.

3. Each child picks up his picture carefully, holds it horizontally, and carries it outside.

   Hold the picture out in the rain, so the drops fall and mix with the blue tempera. The result will be a blotchy, rainy effect. This takes less than a minute. Too much water and your picture will smear and wrinkle. Students place their pictures on their desks (or a safe corner of the classroom) to dry.

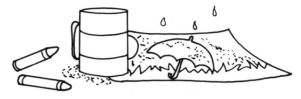

Seasonal Art

The Butterfly Flyer

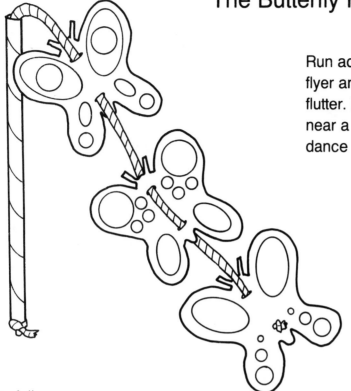

Run across the grass with the flyer and watch your butterflies flutter. Hang it from the ceiling near a window or doorway to dance in the spring breeze.

Materials:

- Butterfly forms - reproduce the pattern below.
- Construction paper squares in spring colors 5" x 5" (13 cm x 13 cm)
- Narrow roving - 32" (82 cm)
- Drinking straws
- Scissors
- Felt pens
- Hole punch
- Pipe cleaners

Steps to follow:

1. Trace around the butterfly pattern on paper squares. Cut on the trace lines.

2. Punch holes on the marked spots.

3. Decorate your butterflies with felt pens.

4. Attach the end of your roving to a pipe cleaner. Using this as a needle, push the roving through the straw. Knot one end of the roving to prevent slippage.

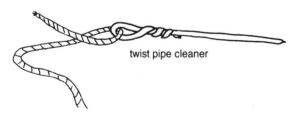

twist pipe cleaner

Now lace the pipe cleaner through the butterflies. Remove the pipe cleaner and knot the end of the roving.

Watch those butterflies spin!

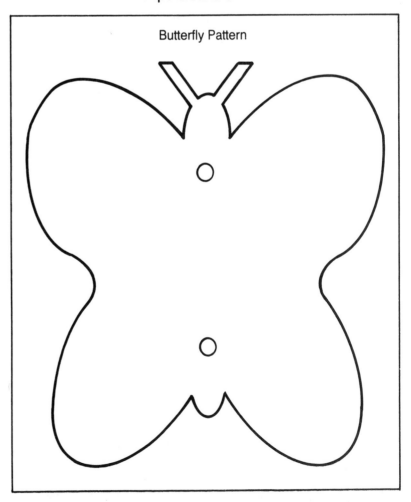

Butterfly Pattern

105

April Showers Bring May Flowers

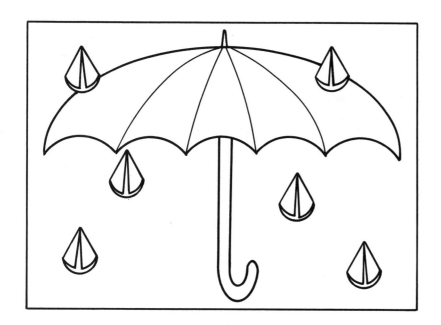

Watch the raindrops turn into flowers as if by magic! Fun for individuals to create or as a class bulletin board project.

Materials:
- Construction paper
  white 12" x 18" (30.5 cm x 45.7 cm) background
  red 18" x 6" (45.7 cm x 15 cm) umbrella
  blue 4" x 4" (10 cm x 10 cm) raindrop/flowers
- Chalk
- Hair spray - to adhere chalk
- Black felt pen
- Scissors, glue

Steps to follow:

1. Cut the umbrella top from red paper.

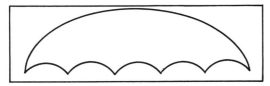

2. Paste the umbrella top to the background sheet.

Use black felt pen to outline the umbrella, make the handle and add curving ribs.

3. Fold blue paper squares and trim.

4. Open the raindrops and create bright flowers inside using colored chalk.

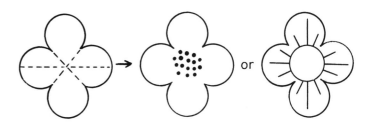

Spray the flowers lightly with hair spray to reduce smearing of chalk.

5. Fold the raindrops back up to hide the flowers and paste them to the background. Make as many raindrops as you wish.

You and your friends can peek at the surprise flowers. It gives new meaning to old saying "April showers bring May flowers".

Thumbprint Geraniums

Create lush geranium blossoms quickly with the most efficient of all tools...fingers!

Materials:
- White art paper 9" x 12" (22.8 cm x 30.5 cm) or 12" x 18" (30.5 cm x 45.7 cm)
- Green construction paper squares for leaves thin strips for stems
- Black crayon
- Paste
- Red tempera in a flat bowl
- Paper towels

Steps to follow:

1. Use black crayon to outline a cloud shape where you intend to place each geranium. Place them in three spots, leaving room for leaves and stems.

2. Fill in the "cloud" areas using your fingertip or thumbprint dipped into the red tempera. Make an uneven number of petals on each flower. You may want to make one smaller to represent a bud.

3. Lay down the green strips. Experiment with placement until you find one you like. Then paste down the stems.

4. Round the edges of the green squares. Cut out a triangle section and scallop the edges to form geranium leaves.

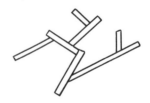

Bend or roll some edges for a three-dimensional look.

Arrange on the stems. Paste down.

A Bird Mobile

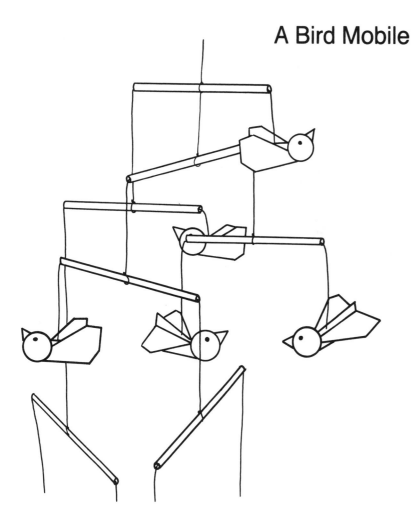

Each child contributes one or two spring birds to this wonderful mobile for your classroom.

Materials:
- Reproduce the pattern on the following page.
- Hole punch
- String or yarn
- Straws
- Felt pens

Steps to follow:

1. Construct the birds according to the step by step directions on the pattern page.

2. Lay out the straws on a table to help in planning your mobile design. Make two or more mobiles if one seems too heavy with birds.

3. Balancing a mobile requires patience! Tie the straws together with yarn or string.

   Place a strip of tape over the tied portion to prevent slipping.

   Pull the string through the straws leaving extra length for tying to the birds.

   After all the birds have a place, hang the mobile and balance the birds by pulling the string back and forth through the straw.

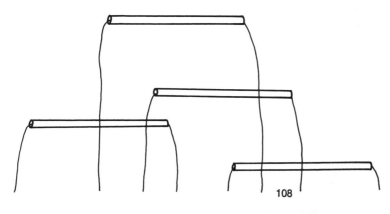

Pattern for Bird Mobile

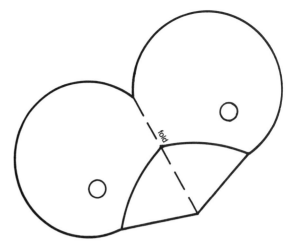

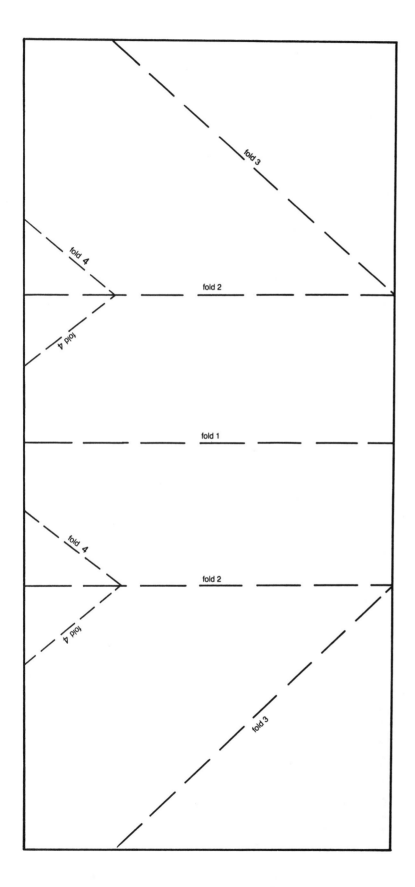

1.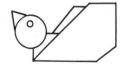

2.

3.

4. ←Fold up and in.

5. Glue on head.

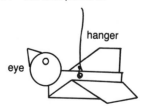

6. Use hole punch for

    eye   hanger

7. Color the bird in bright colors with felt pens. Look in your encyclopedia for ideas of color combinations.

Seasonal Art

Three Dimensional Flowers

Try all of these or experiment with ideas of your own. These are effective additions to cards, bulletin boards, or individual art projects.

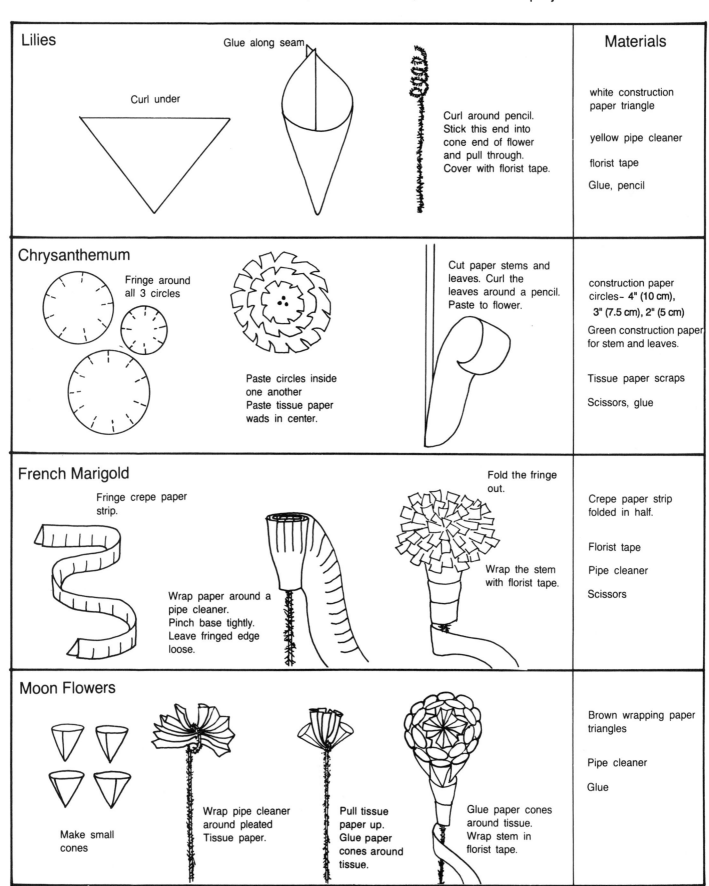

Lilies

Glue along seam

Curl under

Curl around pencil. Stick this end into cone end of flower and pull through. Cover with florist tape.

Materials

white construction paper triangle

yellow pipe cleaner

florist tape

Glue, pencil

Chrysanthemum

Fringe around all 3 circles

Cut paper stems and leaves. Curl the leaves around a pencil. Paste to flower.

Paste circles inside one another Paste tissue paper wads in center.

construction paper circles- 4" (10 cm), 3" (7.5 cm), 2" (5 cm)

Green construction paper for stem and leaves.

Tissue paper scraps

Scissors, glue

French Marigold

Fringe crepe paper strip.

Fold the fringe out.

Wrap paper around a pipe cleaner. Pinch base tightly. Leave fringed edge loose.

Wrap the stem with florist tape.

Crepe paper strip folded in half.

Florist tape

Pipe cleaner

Scissors

Moon Flowers

Make small cones

Wrap pipe cleaner around pleated Tissue paper.

Pull tissue paper up. Glue paper cones around tissue.

Glue paper cones around tissue. Wrap stem in florist tape.

Brown wrapping paper triangles

Pipe cleaner

Glue

Spring Celebration—Window Painting

This project can give your classroom a real lift for spring. (Reassure your custodian that you will be responsible for clean-up!)

Materials:
- Jars of tempera paint
- Paint brushes
- Damp sponges—clean up those spills as soon as they happen.

Steps to follow:

1. Plan your day so the class can work on jobs that allow 4 or 5 to paint at a time. Be flexible so you can supervise classwork and keep an eye on the emerging artwork.

2. Use the chalkboard to form your work plan. Draw an outline of your windows and plan with your students what to paint. (Flower gardens, rainbows, butterflies or "stained-glass" windows all work well.) Let students write their names on what part they will paint.

3. Let all students observe the first group paint as you set up standards and procedures.
   Outline the object you will be painting.
   Fill in details.
   Clean up any paint splats.
   Carefully return paint and brush to a central area.
   Rinse any paint from your sponge.

Cleaning the windows:
Wipe with damp (not wet) paper towels or sponges. It will take several times to completely remove the paint but it is less messy than using large quantities of water. Let everyone take a turn so no one gets too tired. A final wipe with window cleaner and your windows will sparkle like new. 111

Lion and the Lamb

flip

March comes in like a lion and out like a lamb. (Or vice-versa!) Your class will never forget that old saying after they make this "flip-around" puppet.

Materials:
- Paper plates - two 6 1/2" (16.3 cm) plates per puppets
- Tongue depressor
- 1 1/2" (4 cm) orange tissue squares (20 per lion)
- Cotton balls
- Construction paper
  black 1 1/2" x 2 1/2" (4 cm x 6.3 cm) lambs ears
  yellow 1/2" x 1/2" (1.3 cm x 1.3 cm) lion ears
  black 1" x 1" (2.5 cm x 2.5 cm) lambs nose
- Crayons or tempera paint
- Glue

Steps to follow:

1. Lion (use the underside of the plate)
   a. Color the surface with the side of a yellow crayon or paint with yellow tempera paint.
   b. Sketch the face lightly with a pencil. Then trace with a darker color crayon.
   c. Cut the ears from yellow paper. Glue to the plate.
   d. Wrap orange tissue paper squares over a pencil eraser, dip them in glue and set around the edge of the lion's face.

2. Lamb (use the underside of the plate).
   a. Color the lamb's face gray with crayon or paint with tempera paint.

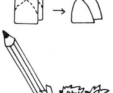

   b. Cut ears from black paper and glue to the plate.
   c. Cut the red nose out and glue in place.
   d. Color the eyes black.
   e. Glue a nest of cotton balls above the ears.
   OPTIONAL: Fluff out more cotton balls and glue below the lamb's chin.

3. Turn the lion and lamb upside down on the table. Place a ring of glue around the top edge of both plates.

   Lay the tongue depressor on one side at the lower mid-point of the puppet. Place the other plate on top and press down until the glue sets.

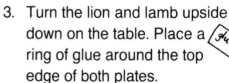

Seasonal Art

Lion and Lamb Patterns

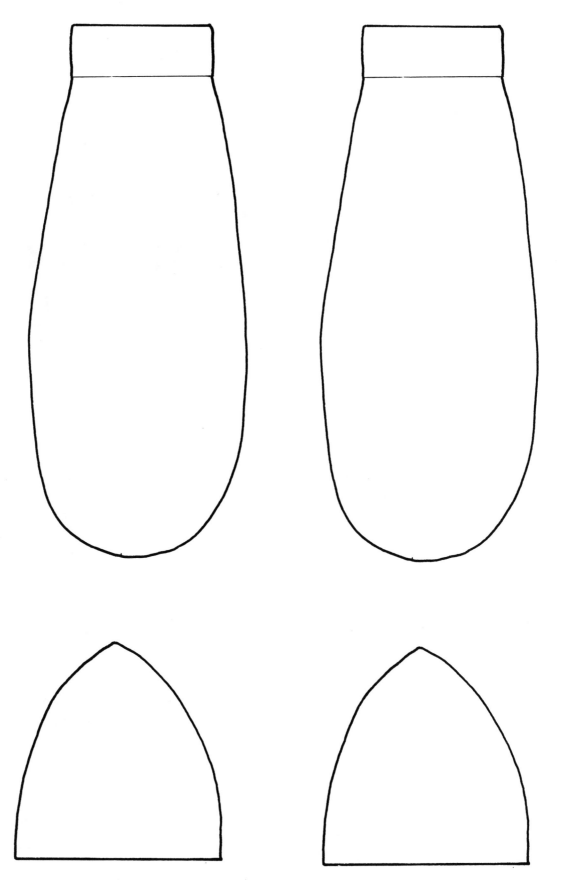

Seasonal Art

Stormy Weather Art

You can almost hear the thunder crack when you look at this one! It offers dramatic textures and effects.

Materials:
- construction paper
  blue-sky
  black-sky line
  yellow-lights in windows
  white-clouds
- glitter (for lightning)
- hole punch
- glue
- scissors
- pencil

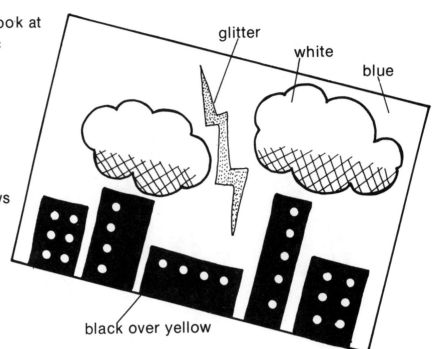

glitter

white

blue

black over yellow

Steps to follow:

1. Establish the skyline with black rectangles. Vary the width and height.
   Punch windows with a hole punch.
   Place a yellow sheet behind each building to shine through the holes as lights. Paste these buildings to the bottom of the blue paper.

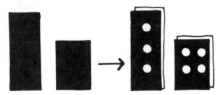

2. Outline the lightning shape with pencil. Fill in the shape with glue. Sprinkle silver glitter over the glue.

3. Cut cloud shapes from white rectangles.
   Add crosshatching for shading (using a pencil) to the lower edge of each cloud.

4. Make the clouds stand out from the background. To do this, cut two strips of white paper for each cloud. (about three inches long) Fold back and forth. Paste to the back of the clouds. Paste the other end to the sky. Now the clouds will stand out!

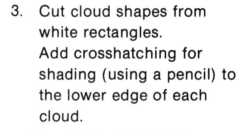

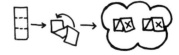

Seasonal Art

Wind Socks

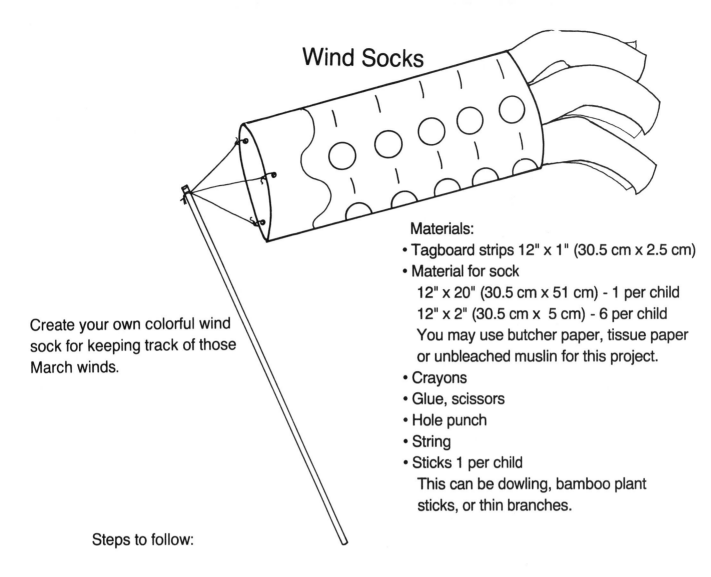

Create your own colorful wind sock for keeping track of those March winds.

Materials:
- Tagboard strips 12" x 1" (30.5 cm x 2.5 cm)
- Material for sock
  12" x 20" (30.5 cm x 51 cm) - 1 per child
  12" x 2" (30.5 cm x 5 cm) - 6 per child
  You may use butcher paper, tissue paper or unbleached muslin for this project.
- Crayons
- Glue, scissors
- Hole punch
- String
- Sticks 1 per child
  This can be dowling, bamboo plant sticks, or thin branches.

Steps to follow:

1. Form a ring by stapling the tag strip.

2. Decorate your material with crayons. If paper, just draw your designs. If cloth, draw your design with wax crayon, cover with newspaper and press with a warm iron to set the color. (Teacher needs to do this for younger students.)

3. Glue wind sock together to form a tube.
   Glue strips to the end.
   Glue the ring inside the front to keep it open.

4. Make 3 holes in the ring end with a hole punch. Tie 15" (38.5 cm) strings to each hole.
   Tie the other end to your stick.

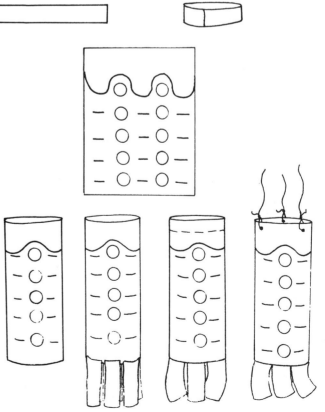

Seasonal Art

Watch the Flower Grow

Pull the tab and your flower grows out of its pot. It's perfect on a greeting card or as an illustration for spring plant stories.

Materials:
- Reproduce the pattern on the following page on construction paper.
- Tongue depressor
- Tissue paper squares
    1" x 1" (2.5 cm x 2.5 cm)
- Construction paper square
    2" x 2" (5 cm x 5 cm)
- Construction paper
    1" x 2" (2.5 cm x 5 cm)
- Crayons or felt pens
- Scissors
- Glue
- Bird Seed—flower center

Steps to follow:

1. Assemble the pattern on the following page.

2. Round the corners of the 2" (5 cm) square

3. Make a ring of tissue flowerettes.

   Wrap the tissue paper squares around a pencil eraser, dip it in glue, and set in place around the construction paper circle.

4. Smear glue in the middle and sprinkle bird seed to form the flower center.

5. Put glue on one end of your tongue depressor. Add the 2" x 1" (5 cm x 2.5 cm) paper strip.

6. Insert the end of the tongue depressor through the slit in your folded page.

   Paste the two outside corners shut.

7. Glue the flower blossom to the top of the tongue depressor.

8. Sketch the flower pot just below the slit.

   Color the background and show leaves coming from the pot.

9. Push the flower down into the pot and then pull it out slowly.

   Watch the flower grow.

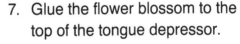

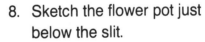

 Seasonal Art

Pattern for Pull Tab Flower

1. Fold on _ _ _ _ _ _ _
2. Cut slit. |—————|

fold
‑ ‑

cut

top

Seasonal Art

A Duck Puppet

These puppets are guaranteed to sing as well as quack. Their favorite songs are *Six Little Ducks That I Once Knew* and *Little White Duck.* Make a flock and sing along!

Materials:
• Reproduce the pattern on the following page.
• Crayons
• Paste
• Scissors

Steps to follow:

1. Color the duck and his beak and eyes.

2. Cut out the head and beak on the dotted lines.

3. Fold the head in half. Cut out the two circles on the fold.

4. Fold the beak sections in half. Paste around the edge of the beak leaving the end open.

5. Insert thumb and index finger through holes in duck's head.

   Slip the beak pockets over your fingers.

   He is ready to sing, quack or tell his story.

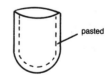

pasted

Seasonal Art

Pattern for the Duck Puppet

Thanks to First Grader Jeff Morgan.

Spring Water Color Flower Garden

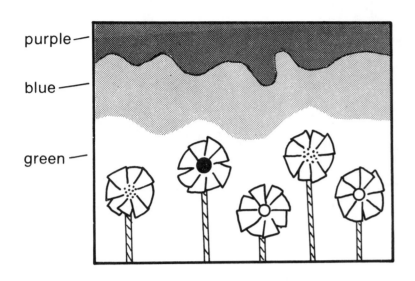

purple —
blue —
green —

This lesson allows students to experiment with watercolor wash and to use the results as a background for a spring landscape.

Materials:
- large white construction paper
- newspapers
- squares of bright colored construction paper
- yarn or roving
- watercolors, brush, cans of water
- one large paint brush and a pail of water

Steps to follow:

1. Place the large white paper on newspapers and dampen it using the large paint brush and pail of water.

2. Begin at the top of the paper using the watercolors. First, use a purple stripe across the top. Let it run down. Then do a blue stripe across the middle, letting it run down. Then do green across the rest of the page. Encourage students to experiment with various mixtures of paint and water, so they can see intensity variations.

3. After the background is dry, cut out the flowers and paste them to the background.

round corners

cut slits   bend up petals

Add yarn or roving for stems.

Seasonal Art

Baby Ducklings

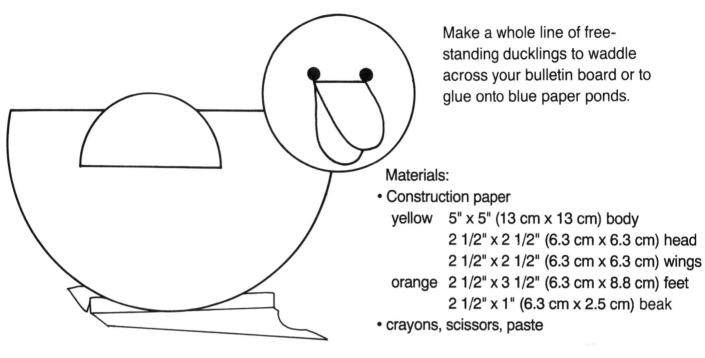

Make a whole line of free-standing ducklings to waddle across your bulletin board or to glue onto blue paper ponds.

Materials:
• Construction paper
  yellow   5" x 5" (13 cm x 13 cm) body
           2 1/2" x 2 1/2" (6.3 cm x 6.3 cm) head
           2 1/2" x 2 1/2" (6.3 cm x 6.3 cm) wings
  orange 2 1/2" x 3 1/2" (6.3 cm x 8.8 cm) feet
           2 1/2" x 1" (6.3 cm x 2.5 cm) beak
• crayons, scissors, paste

Steps to follow:

1. Round off the corners of all yellow pieces.

2. Fold the large yellow circle in half to form the body.

3. Paste one of the small yellow circles on as a head.

4. Cut the other small circle in half. Paste one on each side of the body for wings.

5. Fold the large orange paper in half. Fold end flaps up to create a ridge in the middle. Cut to form duck's feet.

6. Paste this piece to the duck's body for feet.

7. Fold the small orange paper in half. Round the ends to create a beak. Paste to the duck's head.

8. Add eyes with crayons.

   Your ducks are all ready for a swim.

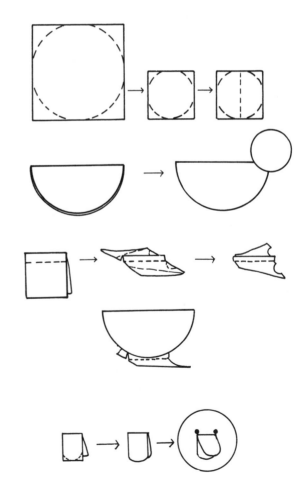

Seasonal Art

Full of Magic and Fun

Spring Pixie Mural

This mural may be large or small; simple or detailed; a group or whole class project. It provides an opportunity for imaginations to soar. The finished product is a great motivator for creative writing.

This mural can be made with whatever materials are available in your school. Butcher paper makes the best background.

Mixed media is very effective. Paint or use felt pens to create the background. Make figures and foliage using tempera paint, felt pens, crayons or construction paper. Cut out and paste to the background.

Any 3-dimensional effects your class can develop will add interest and charm.

Suggested items:

Background foliage:	Characters (3-D is nice!)
Plants with large leaves	Pixies turning cartwheels
Ferns	hanging from vines
Moss	standing still
Mushrooms	asleep
Flowers	Spiders
	Ladybugs
	Dragonflies
	Worms
	Butterflies

Check the encyclopedia for colored pictures of various plant and animal life.

Seasonal Art

Draw Leprechauns

Leprechauns are active little fellows that move quickly. Let's draw them in several positions. Experiment with these poses and discover your favorite one. Maybe you can add a mushroom to house a whole clan of Leprechauns.

Here are the basic poses:

Arms raised in song

Turning a cartwheel

Cross-legged

Dancing a jig

Now add details:

Face

Clothing

Create your own special background.

Seasonal Art

Shamrocks Galore
Potato Prints

• punch 2 holes in the top and lace yarn & tie.

This shamrock bag has a long list of uses:

1. A trap for leprechauns
2. A bag to carry the leprechaun's gold home
3. A special lunch bag for Saint Patrick's Day (take along a snack for the leprechaun!)

Materials:
- Brown grocery bags
- Potatoes
- Knives
- Tempera paint—green white
- Pencils with erasers
- Shamrock cookie cutter
- Saucers

Steps to follow:

1. Slice a potato in half. Press the cookie cutter into the cut end. Trim off the extra potato with a knife.

2. Put puddles of paint in saucers. Dip the shamrock potato into the paint, dab excess off on the paper towel, then press onto bag.

3. Use a pencil eraser dipped in white paint to add dots.

Seasonal Art

The Mischievous Leprechaun

The pieces of this leprechaun's body can be moved around so the student can try different poses for the little fellow.

Materials:
Reproduce the pattern on page 126 for each student.
• Large white drawing paper 12" x 18" (30.5 cm x 45.7 cm)
• Crayons
• Paper scraps and glue (optional)

Steps to follow:

1. Color the pattern pieces. Give the leprechaun an interesting expression. His colthes are green, but use your imagination in adding details.

2. Cut out the pieces Lay the pattern pieces on the large white paper. Experiment until you have a position you like. You can cut on the dotted lines at the elbows and knees if you want to bend them. Paste down the leprechaun.

4. Add details with crayons or paper scraps:.

5. Plan the background.

6. Outlining the leprechaun with black crayon or felt pen adds contrast and definition to the picture.

beard and hair

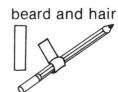

hat

hands

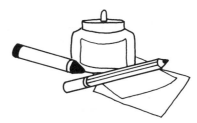

Seasonal Art

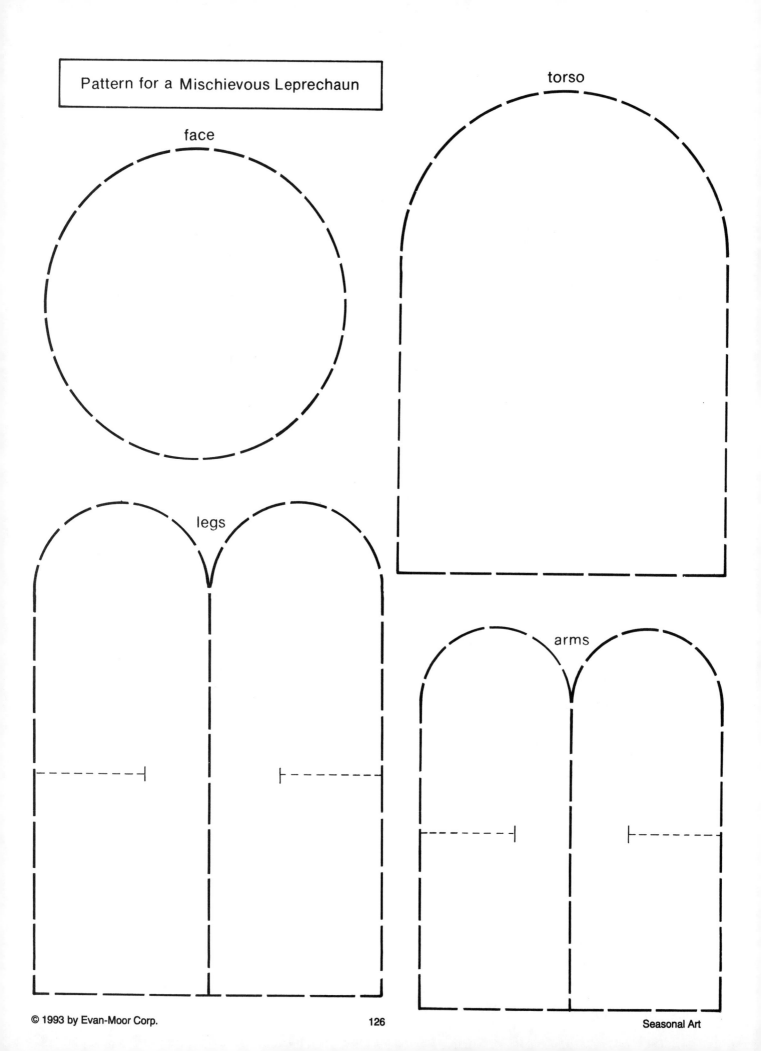

Pattern for a Mischievous Leprechaun

face

torso

legs

arms

Seasonal Art

Natural Egg Dyes

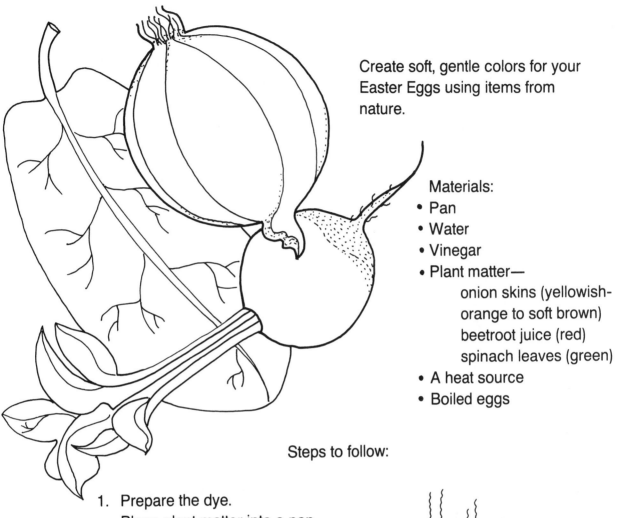

Create soft, gentle colors for your Easter Eggs using items from nature.

Materials:
- Pan
- Water
- Vinegar
- Plant matter—
  - onion skins (yellowish-orange to soft brown)
  - beetroot juice (red)
  - spinach leaves (green)
- A heat source
- Boiled eggs

Steps to follow:

1. Prepare the dye.
   Place plant matter into a pan of cold water. (Prepare dye colors one at a time.) Bring to a boil and simmer gently until you get a good color. Strain and cool.

2. Place eggs in a pan with plant dye. Add a few drops of vinegar. Simmer gently for 30 minutes. Remove eggs from the water. Dry thoroughly. While eggs are still warm, rub with a drop of oil on a cloth to deepen the color.

         Seasonal Art

A Chain of Eggs

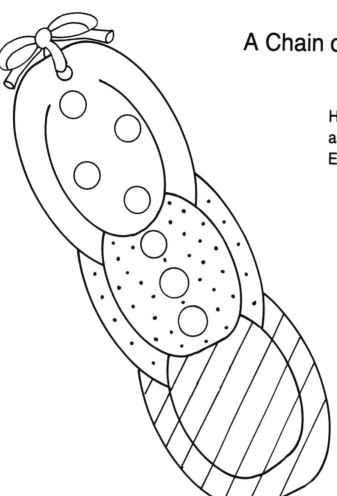

Hang this egg chain on your door as a welcome surprise for the Easter Bunny.

Materials:
- Construction paper
  4" x 3" (10 cm x 7.5 cm)
  6 or more per child
    pink
    yellow
    blue
    lavendar
    orange
    purple
- Colored pencils or crayons
- Scissors
- Hole punch
- Yarn

1. Fold paper rectangles in half. Trace half an egg starting on the fold.

   Now trace another line on the inside of the egg. Stop the line before it makes a complete half circle.

   Cut on the lines . Open the egg.

2. Decorate the eggs with polka dots, stripes, and zig-zags.

3. Loop the eggs together to form your chain.

4. Punch a hole in the top egg and thread a piece of yarn through to form a loop. Tie the yarn in a bow or tassel for extra color.

   Hang your chain and admire your efforts.

Steps to follow:

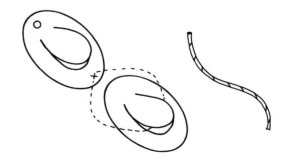

Seasonal Art

Pen and Ink Basket
With Tissue Paper Eggs

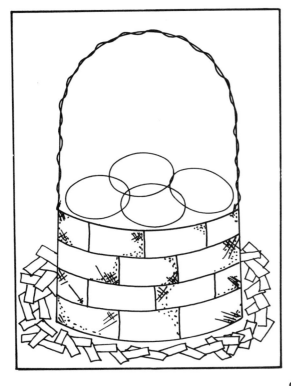

This project requires time and patience. The result is a striking Easter Basket well worth displaying.

Materials:
- White construction paper
  9" x 12" (22.8 cm x 30.5 cm)
- Brightly colored tissue paper
  2 1/2" x 1 1/2" (6.3 cm x 4 cm)
  (about 10 per student)
- Black felt pens - thin line
- Liquid starch in saucers
- Pencils, paint brushes
- OPTIONAL - green tissue paper
  rectangles for grass

Steps to follow:

1. Sketch the basket lightly with pencil on the white construction paper. Encourage students to fill the space.

2. Round the corners on the tissue paper rectangles to create egg shapes.

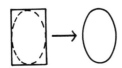

3. Decide where to put the egg in the basket. Place a dab of starch on the spot, lay the tissue egg on the starch; then brush the egg with starch. Repeat this process, overlapping the eggs until your basket is full.

OPTIONAL—Rip green tissue paper into strips and stick to the area below the basket with starch.

Allow the starch to dry completely.

4. Outline the basket and eggs with a fine tip black felt pen.

Showing the basket weave lines and details such as shading with cross-hatching or stippling will add greatly to the final effect.

Seasonal Art

Hatching Eggs

Who is peeking out from your egg? Is it a chick, an alligator, a snake, a bird...?

Materials:
- Construction paper
  background paper in pink,
  blue or spring green
  5" x 3 1/2" (13 cm x 8.8 cm)
  white rectangle - eggs
- Felt pens or crayons
- Scissors, paste

Steps to follow:

Egg shapes can be cut free-hand or from egg pattern forms.

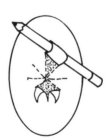

1. Cut egg shapes from white construction paper. Decorate with crayon or felt pens. Use polka dots, stripes, zigzags, or solid colors.

2. Cut the "peel-back" lines on all the eggs. Pull back each section. Press down or curl on a pencil.

3. Paste the eggs to the background sheet.

4. Draw the animal peeking from your egg.

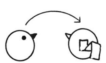

For another effect, try creating a yellow chick (or another animal) from construction paper scraps. Paste it to an accordian pleated strip. Paste the other end of the strip inside the egg. Now the little head of the chick peeks out of the cracked egg.

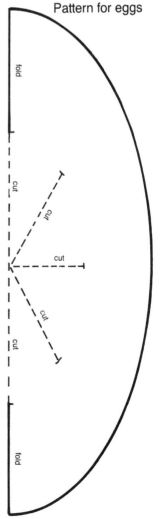

Pattern for eggs

fold

cut

cut

cut

cut

cut

fold

Seasonal Art

Papier Mâché Peek Egg

Peek inside your colorful egg to see a charming Easter or spring scene. This is a time-consuming project, but the end result is worth it.

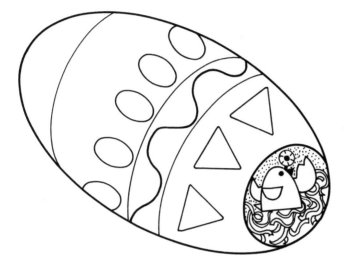

Materials:

Egg—
- Balloons
- Masking tape
- Individual milk cartons
- Newspaper strips
- Wallpaper paste
- Tempera paint
- Brushes

Scene—
- Construction paper scraps
- Felt pens, crayons
- Glue, scissors
- Easter "grass"

Steps to follow:

1. Prepare the balloon.
   Blow up the balloon and tie the end. Tape the balloon to the milk carton.

2. Mix wallpaper paste. Dip strips of newspaper into the wallpaper paste, layng one strip at a time on the balloon. Let strips overlap a little bit. Make the first layer two strips thick. *Let it dry thoroughly.*

   Repeat these steps three times. Let it dry thoroughly each time.

3. When the balloon is dry, cut it free from the milk carton. Trim around the opening and pull out the balloon.

4. Create a colorful design with tempera paint. (Flowers, polka-dots, zig-zags, strips, etc.) Let the egg dry.

5. Create a scene in your egg. Make bunnies, ducks, flowers, Easter eggs and other spring symbols out of construction paper scraps. (Older students may want to use scraps of cloth, ribbon, cotton balls, etc.)

6. Fold a little flap at the bottom of each figure and paste inside the egg.

7. Put Easter grass around your figures. Tuck paper eggs in the grass. (Or jelly bean eggs!)

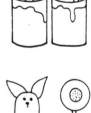

 Seasonal Art

Spring Sponge Painting

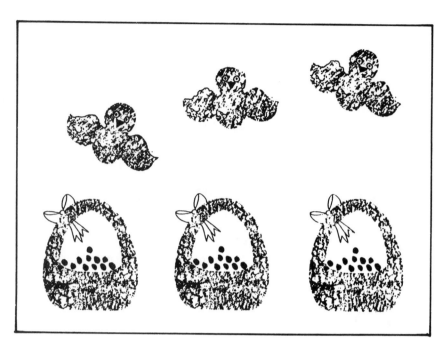

Use this lesson to experiment with colorful designs. Use the finished results to create a bulletin board. Or use individual prints to create Easter cards to share with friends and family.

Materials:
- Sponges
- Scratch paper or old newspapers for practice
- Pencils with erasers
- Tempera paint—colors that contrast with background paper
- Saucers—for paint
- Paper towels
- Construction paper

Steps to follow:

1. Cut sponges into shapes using the patterns provided on the following page. (Adjust the size to suit your needs.)

2. Place puddles of paint in the saucers. Dip sponge in paint, lightly pat on paper towel to remove any excess, then press on paper. Practice on newsprint. When you have a satisfactory design, print on construction paper.

3. Here are some ideas for adding details to your prints.

The Chick or Bird
Add beaks, eyes and legs with crayons.
Birds can be grouped in a row or grouped together in a flock.

The Egg
Use the pencil eraser to add bright designs to your egg. Or add line designs with crayons.

The Bunny
Use a pencil eraser to print a colored eye and nose on the bunny.
Repeat the bunny several times in a row and add "hop" lines with a crayon.
Draw an egg in his paw.

The Basket
After printing the basket, dip a pencil eraser in brightly colored paint and print eggs.

Seasonal Art

Pattern Suggestions for Sponge Painting

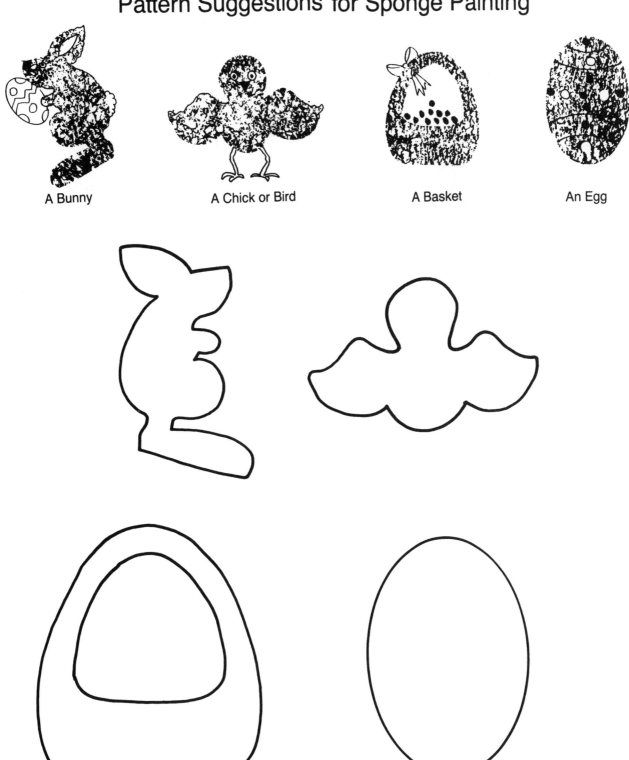

A Bunny   A Chick or Bird   A Basket   An Egg

       Seasonal Art

Easter Centerpiece

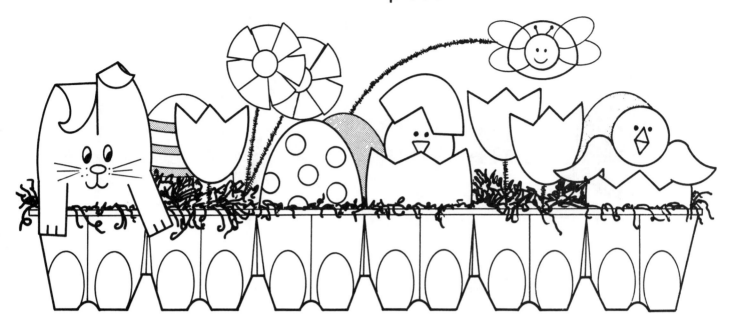

You can create a wonderful centerpiece to send home at Easter time or everyone can construct part of a centerpiece to be used at a school party.

Materials:
- Reproduce the patterns on the following page on construction paper.
- Construction paper—
     assorted sizes
     various colors
- Egg carton base
- Pipe cleaners
- Easter Grass—
     any color
- Glue, paste
- Scissors
- Tape
- Crayons or felt pens
- Paint and brushes

Steps to follow:

1. Paint egg carton base. Let it dry completely.

2. Every centerpiece can be different. Pick and choose the patterns you prefer. Color with crayon or felt pens. Older students may prefer to create their own ideas using scraps of paper, cloth, ribbon, yarn, etc.

3. Glue finished pieces into their egg carton slots. Flowers and bees may hover above the rest if they are put on pipe cleaners. The end of the pipe cleaner can be stuck through the egg carton and taped underneath.

4. Fill in all corners with Easter grass.

P.S. Refrigeration not required!

Seasonal Art

Patterns for Easter Centerpiece

135

Seasonal Art

Paper Bag Bunny Headband

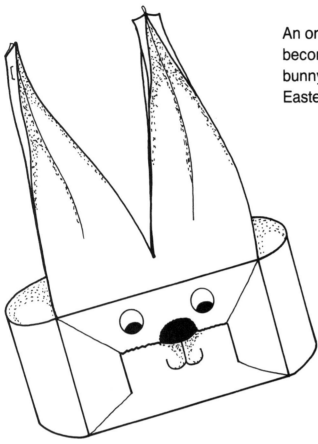

An ordinary, brown lunch bag becomes a wonderful, brown bunny headband to wear in the Easter parade.

Materials:
- Brown lunch bag
- Felt pens or crayons
- Cotton ball
- Scissors, glue
- Stapler

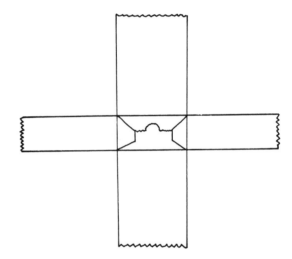

Steps to follow:

1. Cut the paper bag on the side fold lines.

2. Fold up the bottom flap.

3. Cut down the center (both layers) for the ears. Pinch ears together and staple. Cut off excess paper.

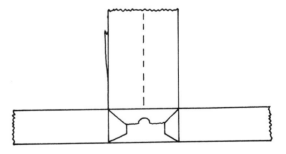

4. Add ears, nose, and other details with felt pens.

5. Fit to child's head and staple headband shut. Add a fluffy cotton ball to the back for bunny's tail.

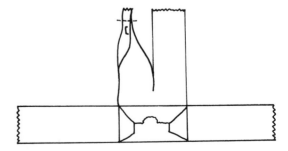

Seasonal Art

A Bunny Box

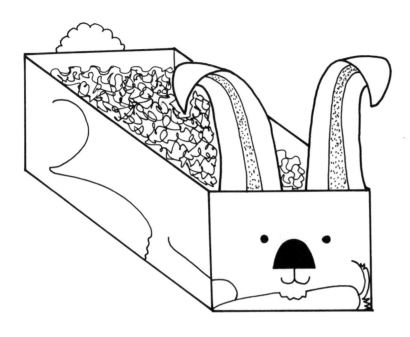

This bunny box is easy to make and very useful as an Easter basket substitute.

Materials:
- Shoebox
- Tempera paint
    white or brown
- Construction paper
    white or brown
    pink
    orange
- Felt pens
- Scissors, glue

Steps to follow:

1. Paint the shoebox white or brown. Let it dry completely.

2. Cut two matching ears from white or brown. Paste a pink strip down the middle. Paste the ears to the box. Bend the ears forward.

3. Use a pencil to lightly sketch in the legs and eyes on the box. Trace over these lines with black felt pen.

4. Cut out of construction paper:
    a pink nose
    a juicy carrot
    a white fluffy tail

    Paste these to your bunny box.

5. Fill the inside of the box with Easter grass. Who knows what might show up on Easter morning?

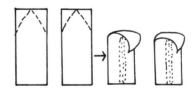

Seasonal Art

Bunny Ear Patterns for Bunny Box

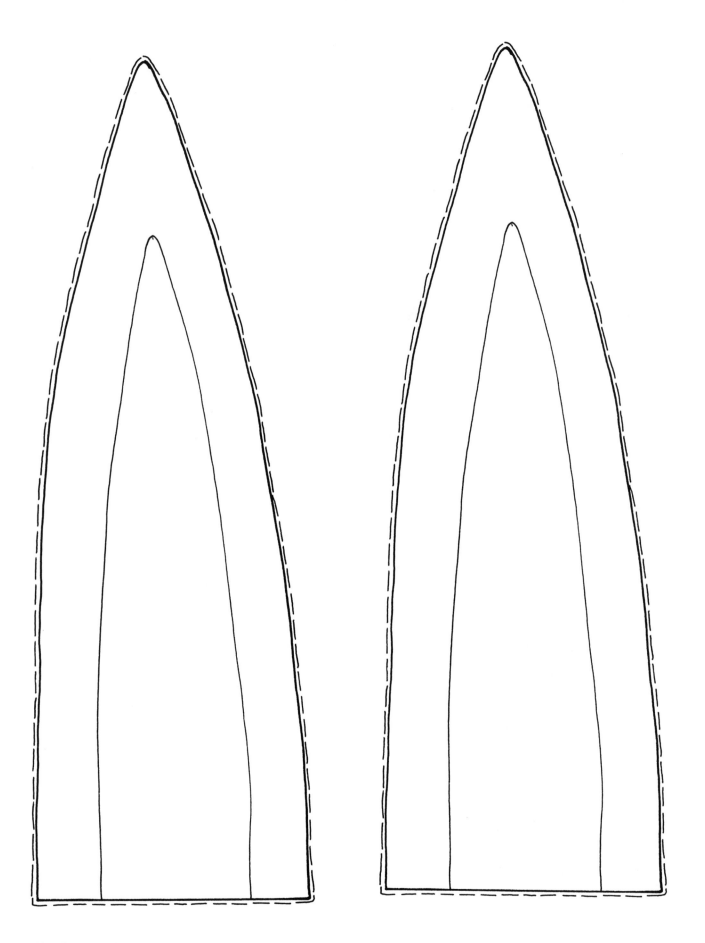

Seasonal Arts

Cut and Paste Rabbit

Here is an easy to make rabbit constructed from basic shapes. Will you make a soft white bunny or a fast-footed brown rabbit?

Materials:
- Construction paper
  blue background
    12" x 18" (30.5 cm x 45.7 cm)
  white/brown
    8" x 5" (20.5 cm x 13 cm) body
    4" x 3" (10 cm x 7.5 cm) head
    3" x 5" (7.5 cm x 13 cm) ears
  green
    18" x 2" (45.7 cm x 5 cm) grass
  pink
    1" x 1" (2.5 cm x 2.5 cm) nose
    4" x 2" (10 cm x 5 cm) inner ear
- Cotton ball
- Felt pens or crayons
- Scissors, paste

Steps to follow:

1. Round the corners on the basic body parts.

2. Lay the pieces in place on the blue background sheet. Decide on the best placement of all the parts. (Leave a space at the bottom for the grass).

3. Cut the green grass across the top side.

   Lay the grass on the background. Adjust the bunny pieces. Paste all parts in place.

4. Cut the pink paper to fit. Paste to the bunny's head.

5. Paste the cotton ball as a fluffy bunny tail.

6. Use crayons or felt pens to add details.

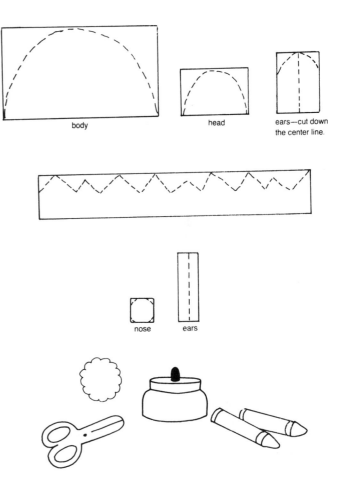

body

head

ears—cut down the center line.

nose   ears

A Chain of Bunnies

Bunny chains are perfect around a bulletin board. They form a charming border on an Easter card. Color both front and back. Let them stand on a table as a centerpiece for Easter dinner.

Materials:
- Construction paper
  4 1/2" x 12" (11.3 cm x 30.5 cm)
- Scissors
- Crayons or felt pens
- Ruler

Steps to follow:

1. Fan fold the 4 1/2" x 12" (11.3 cm x 30.5 cm) paper into 2 1/4" (5.7 cm) segments.

   This is a good time for students to practice measuring skills.

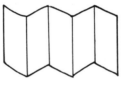

2. Provide students with copies of the tracing template. Students place the bunny shape on the first section of the folded paper.

   Trace around the template.

   Cut on the tracing line.

3. Open the bunny chain to see if they are all connected at their hands and feet. Try again if it didn't work the first time.

4. Now decide how to dress your bunnies. Use crayon or felt pens. Don't forget to show fluffy tails on their back sides.

   You may want to make every other bunny face the opposite

Tracing Template

2¼

must touch fold

must touch fold

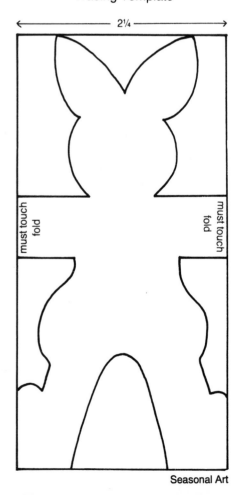

Seasonal Art

Draw Rabbits, Rabbits, Rabbits

Begin by teaching students how to draw the basic rabbit shape.
Then let students explore new ways to portray these busy, little
fellows.

Allow students to practice sketching bunnies many times on a page.
Experiment with size, number, and activity.

Make them large and small.

Make a line of bunnies hopping across a green meadow.

Show them munching a leaf, crunching a carrot, or wiggling little
noses.

Can you change this bunny design into a lovely lop-eared rabbit?

Try moving the legs to create new impressions.

                                                                       Seasonal Art

Chalk Bunnies with 3-D Tails

Create the soft, fuzzy look for these comical bunnies by drawing part of each body with chalk.

✱ *alt. trace stencils w/ chalk*

Materials:
- Construction paper
  blue background
    12" x 18" (30.5 cm x 45.7 cm)
  white
    4" x 4" (10 cm x 10 cm)
        bunny bottom (3)
    1" x 3" (2.5 cm x 7.5 cm)
        spacer bar (3)
- Chalk
- Cotton balls
- Black felt pen or crayon
- Paste and scissors
- Glue
- Hair spray
- Scissors, stapler

Steps to follow:

1. Round the corners of the 4" x 4" (10 cm x 10 cm) white paper.

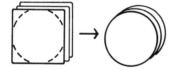

Accordian fold—
Fold the 1" X 3" paper into thirds. Glue one end of the folded strip to the center of the circle. Glue the other end of the strip along the center line of the blue background sheet. Repeat for each bunny.

There will be room for 3 bunnies on the blue sheet.

2. Use chalk to draw the rest of the bunny's body.

3. Use black felt pen or crayon to add eyes, nose, and a big smile.

4. Glue a cottonball to the center of each white circle.

Chalk smearing may be minimized by spraying the whole area lightly with hair spray.

Seasonal Art

Cross Legged Bunny

This whimsical bunny sits up on a desk or table ready to be filled with grass and Easter goodies.

Materials:
- Construction paper
  - white   6" x 6" (15 cm x 15 cm) body
  - 2" x 3/4 (5 cm x 2 cm) 4 per child for ears and arms
  - red   1" x 1" (2.5 cm x 2.5 cm) nose
- Felt pens
- Cotton balls
- Scissors, stapler

Steps to follow:

1. Fold the 6" x 6" (15 cm x 15 cm) paper.

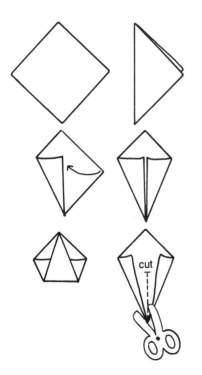

2. Cut and paste to the body

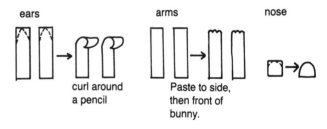

ears

curl around a pencil

arms

Paste to side, then front of bunny.

nose

3. Color:
   - basket—brown
   - eyes—black
   - ears—a pink strip down the middle

4. Cross the bunny's legs. Staple at the base. Pull out the pocket and staple.

5. Glue a cotton ball on behind.

Bunny Pop-Up

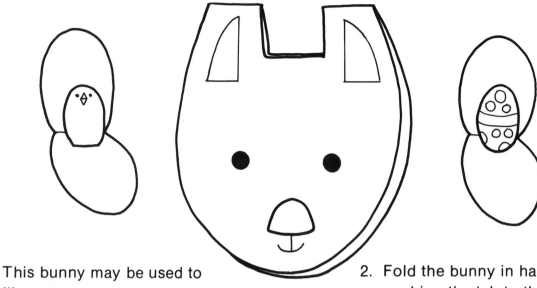

This bunny may be used to illustrate a story or as an Easter card to send home to parents.

Run a copy of the pattern on page 145 for each child. Use construction paper. Brown or white bunnies are both charming.

Steps to follow:

1. Cut out the bunny pattern. Cut on all dotted lines. (Teachers of very young students may need to cut the center lines before passing out the forms.)

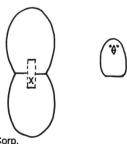

2. Fold the bunny in half, pushing the tab to the inside of the shape.

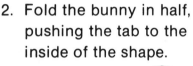

3. Using crayons or paper scraps, create the bunny's face.

4. Color the little chick. Open the bunny and paste the chick inside. Put the paste on the tab only where the chick will touch. (This is marked with an X on the pattern.)

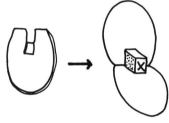

If you prefer, use the egg instead of the chick as your pop-up surprise.

Seasonal Art

Bunny Pop-Up Pattern

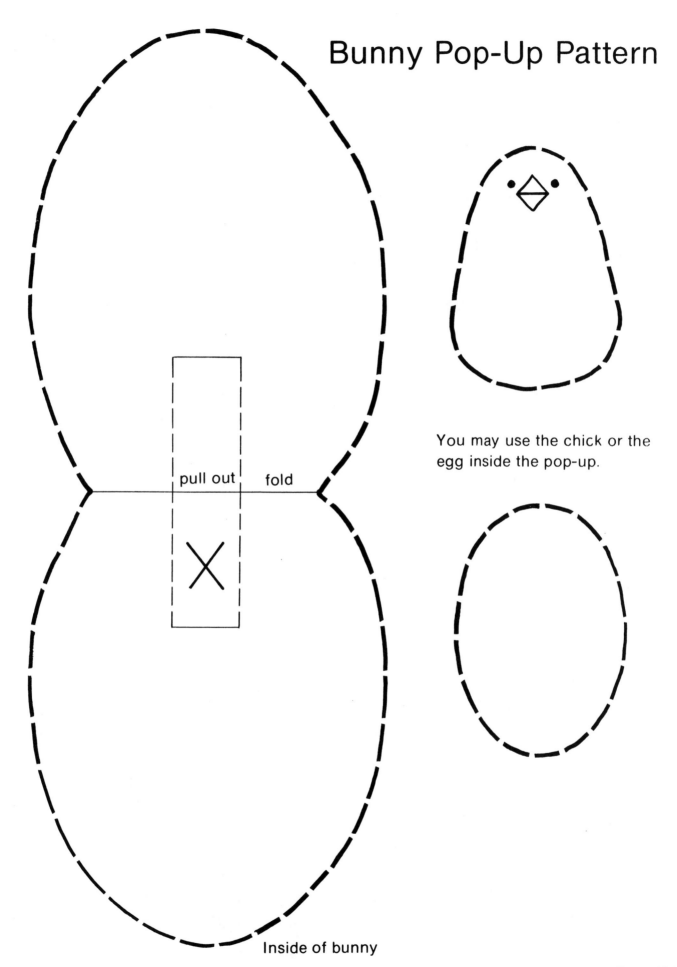

pull out | fold

Inside of bunny

You may use the chick or the
egg inside the pop-up.

Seasonal Art

A May Basket

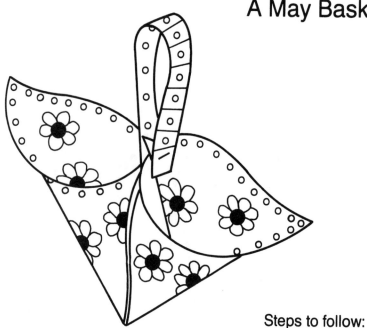

Fill this great little basket with spring flowers and leave it on a friend's door on May 1st.

Materials:
• Construction paper
    9" x 12" (22.8 cm x 30.5 cm)
        any bright color
• Scissors
• Stapler
• Hole punch (OPTIONAL)
• Crayons

Steps to follow:

1. Cut a 3" (7.5 cm) piece off the 9" x 12" (22.8 cm x 30.5 cm) construction paper. Save the smaller piece for a handle.

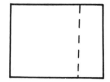

2. Fold the square section into quarters.

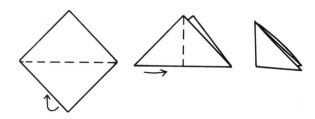

3. Open the folded paper. Use crayons to color bright flowers all over both sides of the square. OPTIONAL: Use a hole punch around the edge to give it a lacy look.

4. Place an index finger in the center and press down firmly. Pull up the two corners that border the fold. Cross over the ends and staple.

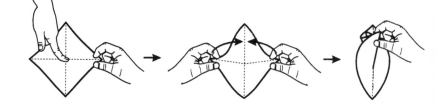

5. Fold the handle piece.

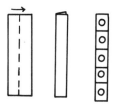

Color flowers, dots or stripes to add interest. You can use the hole punch here, too.

6. Fold the handle over the stapled basket ends. Staple again through all layers.

Seasonal Art

A Calaveras Jumping Frog

You can have your own classroom frog jumping contest when this activity is complete. Graph how far each frog jumps or write a story about each frog's special talents.

Materials:
- Lightweight paper
  9" x 4" (22.8 cm x 10 cm)
  typing paper
  origami paper or
  duplicating paper
- Crayons
- Scissors, glue
- Scrap paper - eyes and tongue

Steps to follow:

1. Fold the paper:

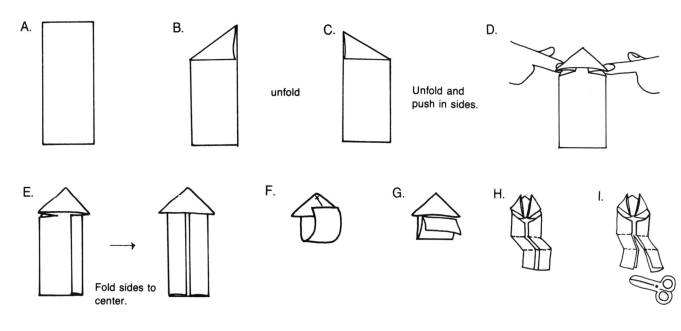

A.

B.

unfold

C.

Unfold and push in sides.

D.

E.

Fold sides to center.

F.

G.

H.

I.

2. Color your frog.
   Check the encyclopedia for frog colorations.

3. Cut eyes from scrap paper.
   Glue in place. Some frog lover may want to add a tongue too!

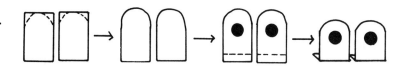

Seasonal Art

A Trainload of Wishes for Mom

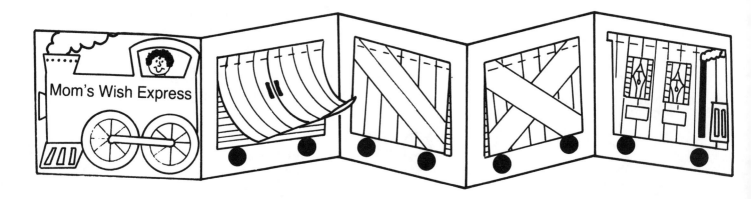

Materials:

- Accordian fold paper for basic card form. Each segment is 6" x 5" (15 cm x 13 cm). Use construction paper, butcher paper or tagboard.

- Reproduce patterns on the following pages.

- 5" x 3" (13 cm x 7.5 cm) sheets of writing paper (4 per train)

- black construction paper 1" (2.5 cm) squares for wheels (8 per train)

- felt pens

- scissors, paste

Steps to follow:

1. Assemble the accordian folded basic card shape.

2. Color and cut out the engine, car and caboose patterns. Each child draws a picture of themselves in the engineer's seat.

3. Round the corners on the 1" black squares for wheels. □ ➔ ○

4. Paste:

    a. engine - paste it on the first segment of the card. Add smoke coming from the smokestack.

b. writing paper - paste it in the next four segments.

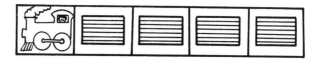

c. wheels - paste below the writing paper.

e. caboose - paste it on the last segment.

d. car doors - paste over each piece of writing paper.

Patterns for Mom's Trainload of Wishes

Mom's Wish Express

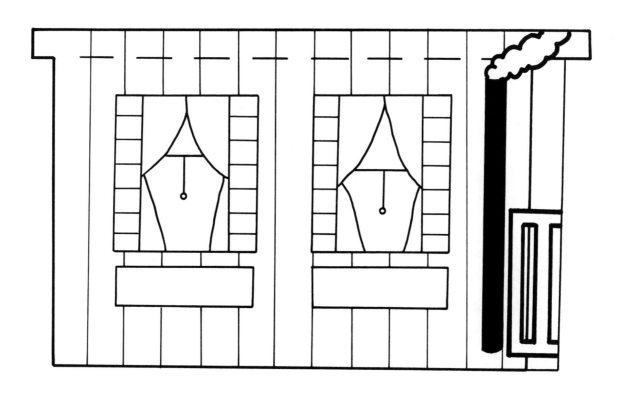

Seasonal Art

Patterns for Mom's Trainload of Wishes

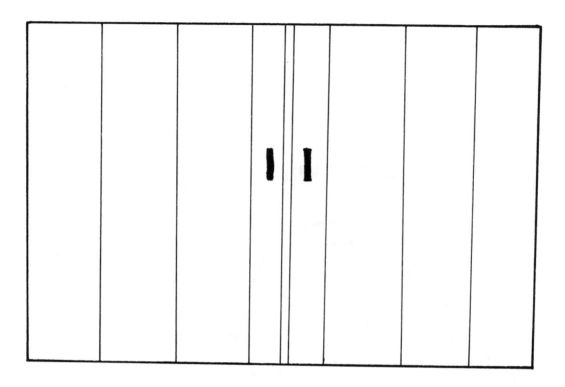

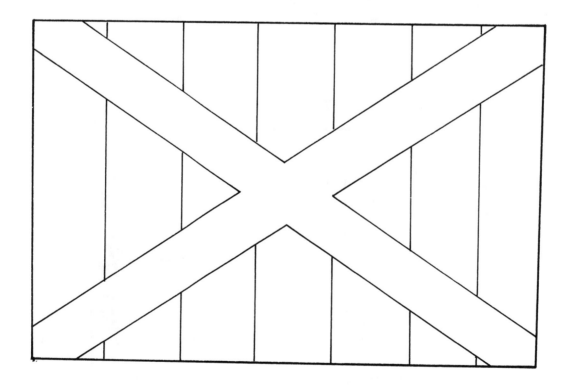

Seasonal Art

Father's Day Card

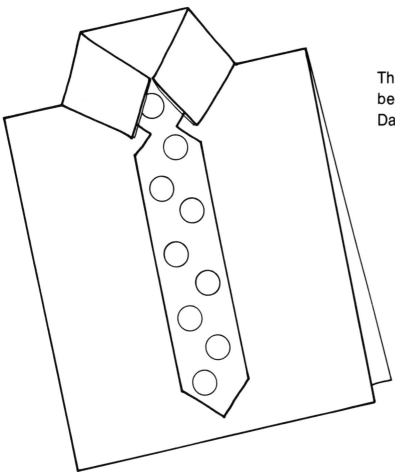

This simple shirt and tie opens to become a clever greeting card for Dad's special day.

Materials:
- Construction paper
  white
      11" x 4 1/2" (28 cm x 11.3 cm) for shirt
  various colors
      1 1/4" x 4" (3.2 cm x 10 cm) for tie
- Ruler, pencil
- Scissors, paste

Steps to follow:

1. Fold white paper in half to form shirt. Measure down 1" (2.5 cm) from the fold. Make a dot. Draw a 1 1/2" (4 cm) line in from the dot. Cut on the line.

2. Fold in at an angle to form the collar.

   Cut a tie from the colored strip.

   Paste to the shirt.

   Open the shirt and write a special Father's Day message for your dad.

Seasonal Art

Summer

Underwater Scene

The ocean may be too far from where
you live for a visit, but you can bring
some "sea breezes" into your classroom
with a few materials and some creative
thinking. Display the finished plates on a
bulletin board so that students and
parents can admire the different scenes.

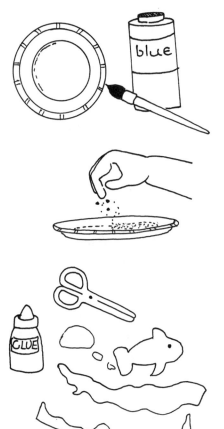

Materials:
• large paper dinner plate
• blue tempera paint mixed with a little liquid soap
• sand
• small rocks and pebbles
• construction paper in assorted colors
• Saran Wrap
• tape and white glue
• scissors

Steps to follow:
1. Paint the front of the paper plate with the blue tempera paint.
If the plate has a plastic covering or finish, add liquid soap to
the paint before using it.

2. While the paint is still wet, sprinkle sand over the lower third
of the plate.

3. Cut or tear fish and other sea animals, shells, rocks and
plants from construction paper. Place these in the scene. Glue
everything in place. (Use real bits of shell and dried kelp if
available.)

4. Attach small rocks or other 3-dimensional items with glue.

5. Stretch Saran Wrap over the front of the plate to complete
the picture of a glossy underwater view. Secure the Saran
Wrap to the back of the plate with a few strips of tape.

Sandcasting

This activity is the most fun if done at the beach, of course! However, a sandbox or a plastic tub full of sand works just as well. This can be messy so smocks and a well-covered floor are a good idea.

Materials:

- sand
- large plastic tub
- plaster of Paris
- small shells, pebbles, driftwood
- spoons
- bucket or can for mixing plaster of Paris
- water
- clean stiff paint brush
- large paper clips (optional)
- water

Steps to follow:

1. Moisten the sand (damp, not wet). Using hands and spoons, form a design in the sand. Don't make it too deep or too large, otherwise it will take forever to dry. A couple of inches (5 cm) deep and six inches (15 cm) or so wide is a nice size. Simple shapes such as a starfish, scallop shell, sun, or fish work best.

2. Add details by drawing in the sand. You may also place shells, pebbles and/or bits of driftwood in the hole to form part of your design.

3. Mix plaster of Paris according to the directions on the package. Pour the liquid plaster into the hole, filling it just to the surface. Let the sandcasting dry undisturbed. The drying time will depend on how large a sandcasting has been made.

If you wish to hang the sandcastings, add a large paper clip "hook" when the sandcasting has set somewhat, but before it has dried completely.

4. Lift the dry sandcasting carefully from the sand. Brush off the excess sand and admire your wonderful creation!

　　　　　　　　　　　　Seasonal Art

The Woolly Lamb

Little Bo-Peep had to wait for her errant sheep to come home. Your students don't have to wait.   They can have a flock of their own ready for the county fair in no time   Just follow these simple directions.

Materials:
- pattern on page 158
- 9" x 6" (22.8 x 20.5 cm) black construction paper
- cotton
- glue
- scissors
- hole punch
- pencil

Steps to follow:
1. Cut out the pattern.

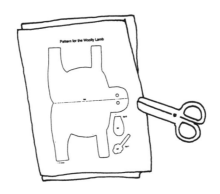

2. Trace around the pattern on the black construction paper. Cut it out.

3. Punch a hole for the eye of the lamb.

4. Smear a thin layer of glue over the body of the lamb. Stretch a layer of cotton over the glued area.

5. Use paper and cotton scraps to make the ears, nose and tail.

Seasonal Art

Pattern for the Woolly Lamb

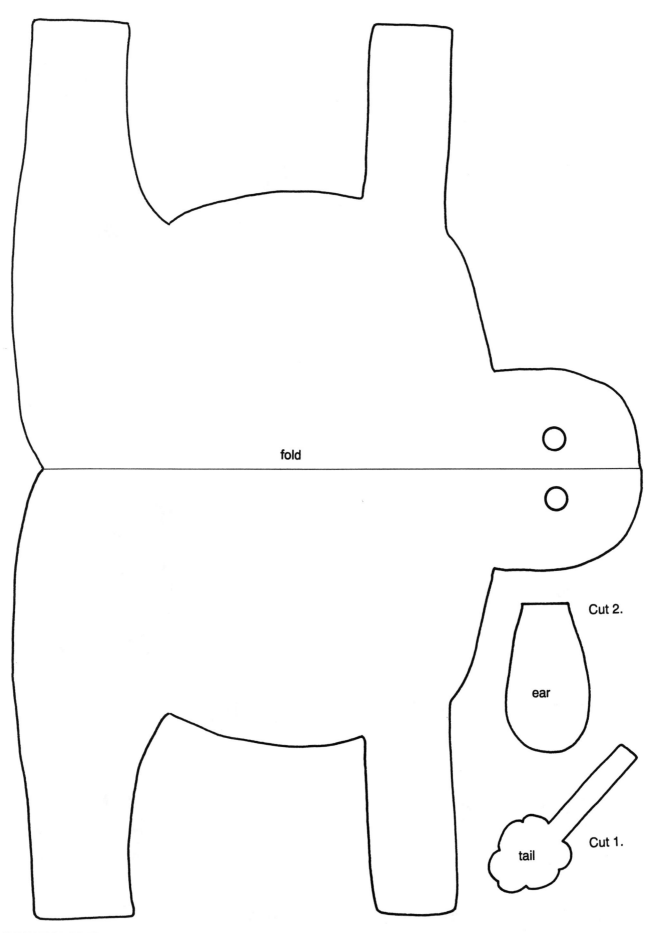

fold

Cut 2.

ear

Cut 1.

tail

Seasonal Art

Prints from Nature

With a little practice, children can create beautiful works of art using items they find in nature. You may want to take a quick walking "field trip" around the neighborhood to collect items to use in this activity. If you do fish prints, be sure to keep the fish on ice when not being used. The materials list recommends construction paper. If your budget is tight, use brown paper bags and newspapers for practice or for the final print. The results may surprise you.

Materials:
• items from nature (fish, shells, wood pieces, etc.)
• 12" x 18" (30.5 x 45.7 cm) construction paper in a variety of colors
• tempera paint
• brayer and large plate
• felt pens
• paper towels

Steps to follow:

1. Go on a nature walk or bring from home a collection of items that have an interesting textured surface that is fairly flat. Be sure the surface of the item used for the printing is dry and clean to start with.

2. Offer students a selection of paint and paper that are contrasting colors...black paper and white paint, blue paint and yellow paper, etc.

3. Put a small amount of paint on a large plate.
Roll the brayer in the paint until it is completely coated.

4. Roll the brayer over the textured area of one of the items.

5. Press the paint-covered area onto the construction paper.
Repeat as many times as desired to create an interesting design.

6. Your students may wish to carry the project one step farther and add details with felt tip pens.

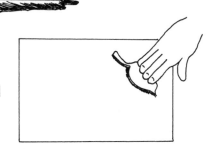

Super Sun Visor

Make this jaunty visor to protect your eyes from the sun on those hot, hot summer days! Add colorful designs and clever sayings to add some fun to your summer attire.

Materials:
- 1/2 of a large paper dinner plate
- (2) 1 1/2" x 12" (3.8 x 30.5 cm) strips of construction paper
- two paper fasteners
- one large rubber band
- scissors and a stapler
- felt tip pens

Steps to follow:

1. Cut out a scoop of the paper plate so that it fits up against the forehead like a visor.

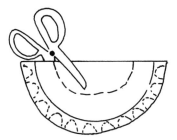

2. Use felt pens to decorate this visor with bright colorful designs.

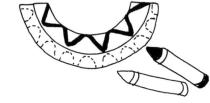

3. Fold the paper strips in half. Double staple the strips to the ends of the visor.

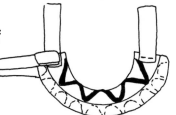

4. Stick the paper fasteners in the end of each paper strip. (You may want to use hole reinforcers to make the visor sturdier.)

5. Loop the rubber band securely around the two paper fasteners.

Seasonal Art

Origami Fox

You never know what you will see while hiking through the woods. If you are really observant (and lucky) you might see one of this fellow's cousins. Keep a sharp eye out for that pointed nose and bushy tail!

Materials:
- red construction paper
  - 6" (15 cm) red square for the fox's body
  - 3" (7.5 cm) red square for the fox's head
- white chalk
- black crayon or felt pen

Steps to follow:
1. Fold the paper for the head.

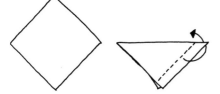 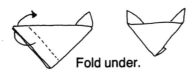

Fold under.

2. Add the details with a black crayon or felt pen.

3. Fold the paper for the body.

Open and refold to the center.

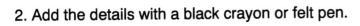

Fold in half.

4. Use white chalk to make a tip on fox's tail.

5. Paste the head to the body.

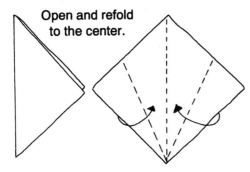 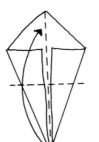 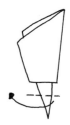 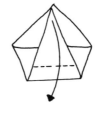 

Your students may want to create a den for their fox out of a shoe box.
They may also want to make smaller versions of the fox to resemble kits
and place them with the mother fox in the den.

Seasonal Art

My Summer Collection Banner

Have you ever returned from a hike or trip with a bag of "stuff" you've collected and now are faced with deciding what to do with it? Here is one way to save the collection in an interesting way.

Materials:
• a large brown grocery bag
• a wire hanger
• 9" x 12" (22.8 x 30.5 cm) sheets of several colors of construction paper
• shells, rocks, leaves, etc., collected by students
• stapler, scissors and felt pens
• white glue

Steps to follow:

1. Cut down one side of the brown bag. Cut the bottom piece out of the bag.

2. Fold the corners of one end of the bag around the sides of a wire hanger. Staple in place.

3. Design a name plate for the top of the collection banner.

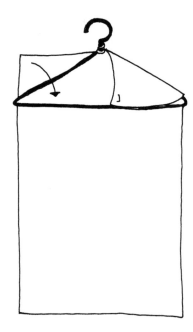

4. Tear hunks of colored construction paper into interesting shapes. Space them around the banner. When you like the arrangement, glue the pieces to the brown bag.

5. Glue your collected treasures to the construction paper.

Seasonal Art

County Fair Merry-Go-Round

What can be more fun than a day at the county fair? Seeing the exhibits, eating cotton candy and going on the rides...all these make it an exciting summer experience. Hop aboard this merry-go-round and remember the fun!

Materials:
- 2 large dinner size paper plates
- a toilet paper tube
- copy of patterns on pages 164-5 (run these on construction paper or card stock)
- a large size paper fastener
- scissors, hole punch
- white glue
- crayons or felt pen

Steps to follow:

1. Put the two plates together back-to-back and insert the paper fastener in the center. Rotate the plates so that they move around easily.

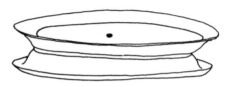

2. Put a puddle of white glue on a piece of paper. Press the end of the toilet paper tube into the glue and then set the tube, glued edge down, on the center of the paper plate.

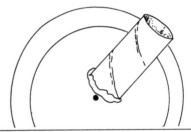

3. Color, cut out and assemble the merry-go-round animals.

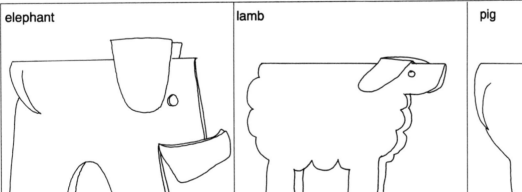

elephant   lamb   pig

4. Color, cut out and assemble the merry-go-round top. Glue it on top of the toilet paper tube.

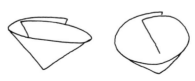

5. Set the animals on the completed merry-go-round. Turn the plate and watch them move.

       Seasonal Art

Merry-Go-Round Animals

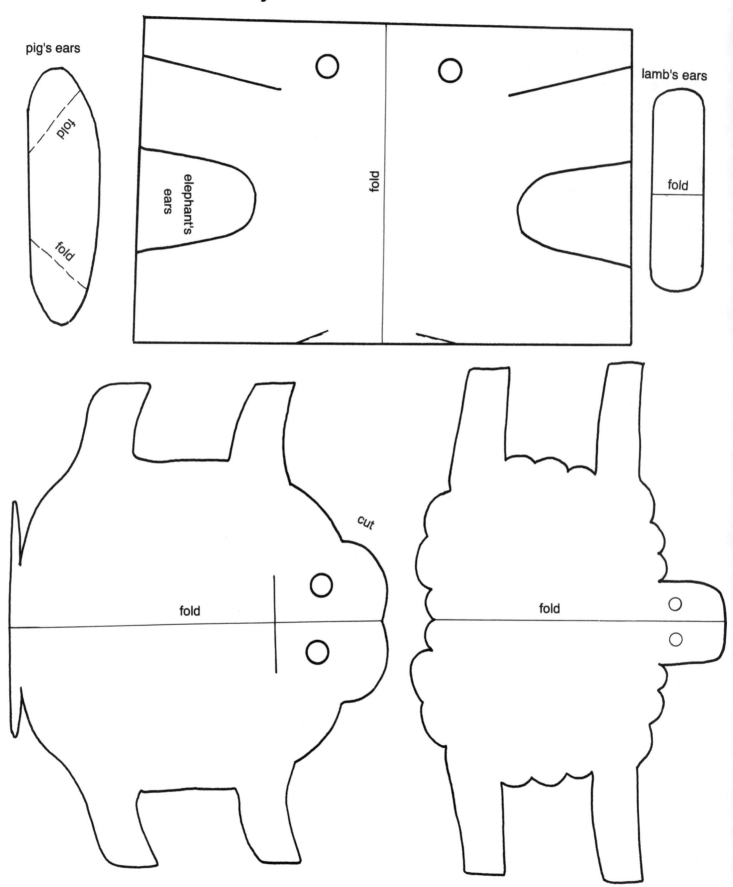

pig's ears

lamb's ears

elephant's ears

fold

fold

cut

Seasonal Art

Merry-Go-Round Carousel

Cut it out.

Roll the circle into a cone shape.

Paste it in place.

Glue onto the top of the toilet paper roll.

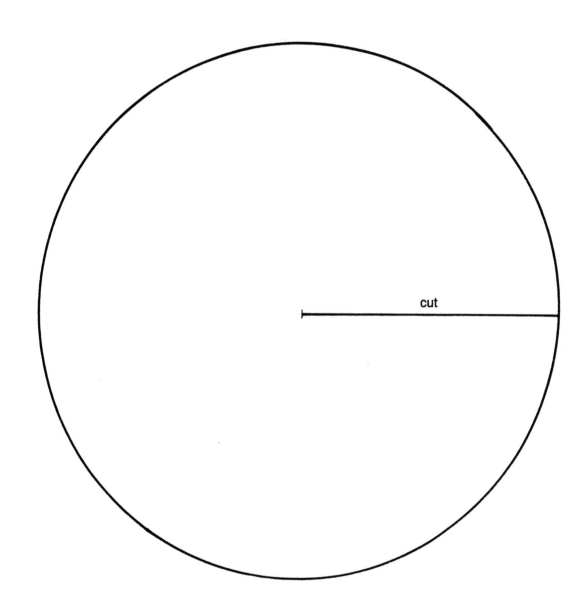

cut

Clowns on Parade

Did the circus ever come to your town on a hot summer day? Maybe there was even a parade of animals and clowns. If not, here is your chance to create your own parade of funny clowns.

Steps to follow:
1. Color and cut out the tent pattern.

2. Cut the slit lines on the tent. Thread the long, narrow strip of construction paper through the slits.

3. Paste the top and the bottom of the tent to the large sheet of construction paper. Be careful not to paste the pull-through strip.

Materials:
• a copy of the tent pattern on page 167
• white construction paper
  12" x 18" (30.5 x 45.7 cm) for the background
  4" x 18" (10 x 45.7 cm) for the pull-through strip
• scissors, crayons and paste

4. Students follow the clown drawing steps shown below, drawing the clown over and over along the strip until they have a parade of clowns. Encourage them to experiment with different postures and expressions on their clowns.

5. Add a background with crayon all around the tent pattern. Is this circus visiting in a city or is it in the country? Are there people lined up to get into see the show?

How to draw a clown:

Move the arms and legs in any direction.

Circus Tent Pattern

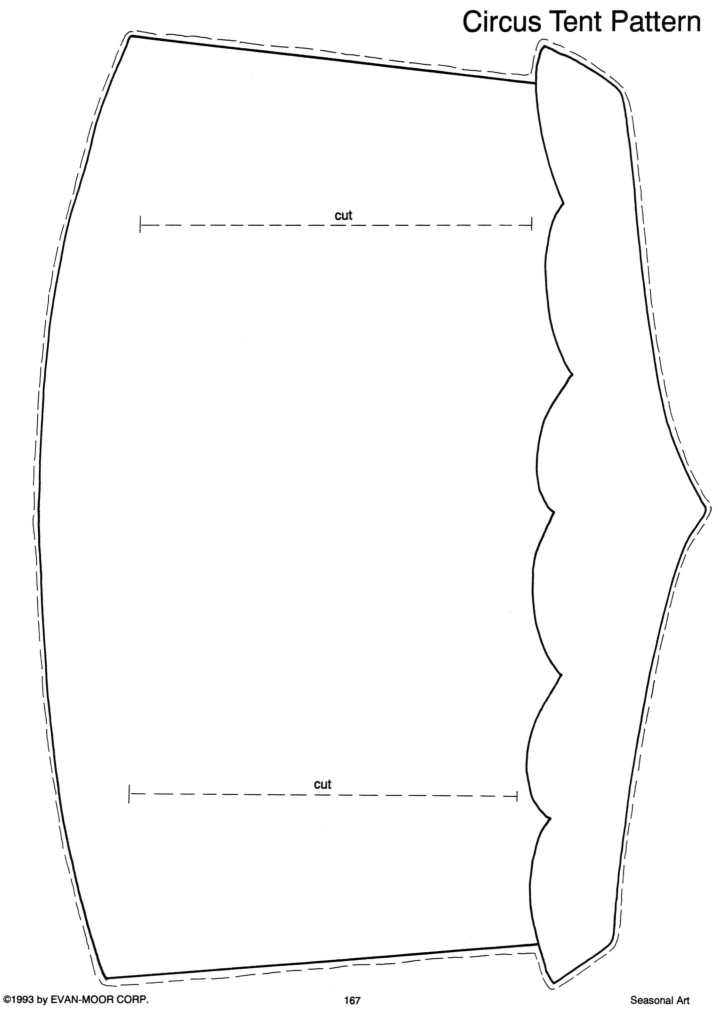

cut

cut

Seasonal Art

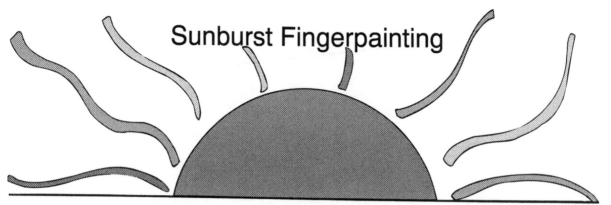

Sunburst Fingerpainting

Fingerpainting doesn't have to be a mess. Set up a few rules in the beginning, then turn your students loose with bright red and yellow to create the warmth of a summer sun.

Materials:
• fingerpainting paper
• red and yellow tempera paint
• liquid starch
• paper towels
• newspapers

Hints:
1. Have children turn their chairs around with the back to the table. The child then stands behind the chair seat. This puts distance between the front of their clothes and the paint.
2. Have an extra paper towel on the seat of the chair. When they are finished they can wipe the excess paint off of their hands so they don't drip on the way to the sink.
3. Establish "washing up" rules before you begin.
4. Fingerpaint the last period of the day and the papers can be left on the desks to dry overnight.

Steps to follow:

1. Place newspaper in front of each student on his or her desk or a table. Place fingerpaint paper on top of the newspaper. Place a paper towel next to the paper so that the student is ready to catch any spills.

2. Put a puddle of liquid starch in the center of the paper. Put a glob of yellow tempera paint in the center of the puddle of starch. Mix the starch and the paint to cover the entire surface of the paper.

3. Add a glob of red paint to one corner of the fingerpaint paper. Begin to mix the red with the yellow background. Watch what happens as the colors mix. Students love to watch the color orange appear as the two colors mix together.

4. Encourage students to try many different techniques in their painting as they explore wavy lines, angular lines, dotted lines, smears, etc.

5. The students may create a sunburst design as a final print.

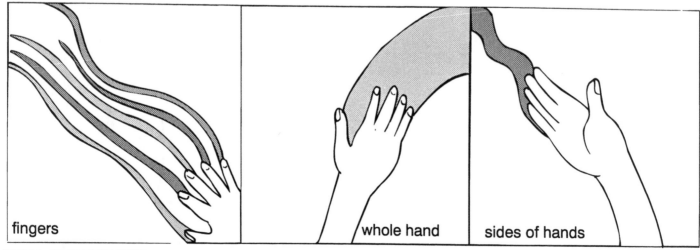

fingers   whole hand   sides of hands

                                       Seasonal Art

Let's Have a Picnic

Fill this basket with great things to eat and head for your favorite picnic spot. Or at least imagine yourself at the park, in the woods, by the lake, at the beach...wherever you'd like to be. Don't forget to pack a little extra for the ants!

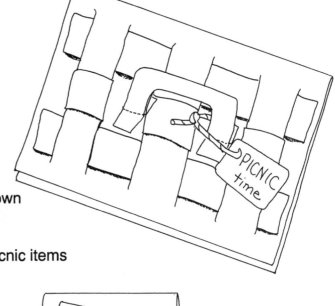

Materials:
• construction paper
    (1) 12" x 18" (30.5 x 45.7 cm) sheet of light brown
    (4) 2" x 12" (5 x 30.5 cm) strips of dark brown
    (1) 6" x 8" (15 x 20.5 cm) piece of light brown
    sheets in various colors and sizes to use for picnic items
• scissors, hole punch and felt pens
• paste
• small strip of yarn
• ruler

Steps to follow:
The Basket
1. Fold the large sheet of light brown construction paper in half. Measure a 1" (2.5 cm) frame all the way around.

2. Measure and mark 2" (5 cm) spaces along the frame. Use the ruler to draw lines at those intervals. Cut on the lines.

3. Weave the dark paper strips in and out through these spaces. Paste the strips in place.

4. Cut a handle for the picnic basket out of the small piece of light brown construction paper. Paste the handle on the top of the woven section.

5. Use the piece you just cut out of the center of the handle and make a tag for your basket with your name on it. Punch a hole in the corner and attach the tag to the handle with a piece of string or yarn.

The Picnic
1. Plan what food you will pack in the basket: sandwiches, chips, fried chicken, etc. Draw these items close to real-life size on appropriate colors of construction paper.

2. Cut or tear out the food shapes and paste them inside the picnic basket. Add details with felt tip pens.

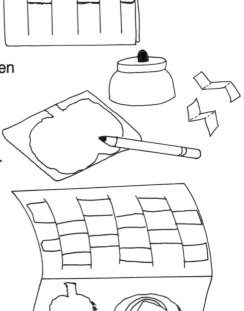

Seasonal Art

Pop-Up Surfer

Surf's Up! Grab your board and head for the beach.

Materials:
- a copy of the patterns on pages 171 and 172
- a sheet of 9" x 12" (22.8 x 30.5 cm) construction paper
- scissors
- felt pens or crayons
- glue

Steps to follow:

1. Color and cut out the surfer and the wave patterns.

2. Fold the pop-up form and cut as instructed.

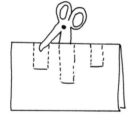 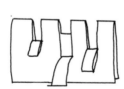 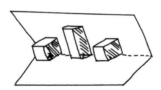

3. Color the background on the pop-up form. Students may want to add fish in the water, other surfers on the horizon, etc.

4. Fold the construction paper sheet in half. Put a row of glue along the outside edge of the back of the pop-up form. Set the glued pattern form inside the folded construction paper. Press closed. Open up the folder and pull the tabs forward.

5. Put a spot of glue on the front part of each of the tabs. Paste the wave piece against the glue on the shorter tabs.

6. Set the surfer against the glue on the tall tab. Fold the surfboard up so that it rests on the shorter tabs.

7. Press the folder closed. Open it again and watch the surfer pop up.

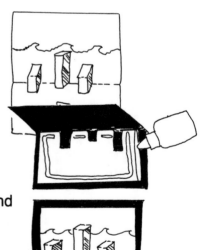

     Seasonal Art

Surfer and Wave Pattern

fold

Seasonal Art

Pop-Up Form

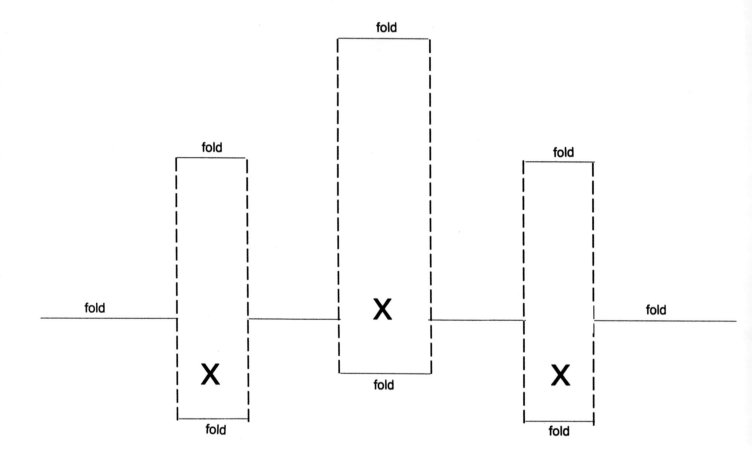

Seasonal Art

Fireworks Light Up the Sky

Fireworks are always exciting. Watching the flashes of color exploding across the sky, then sparkling "stars" drifting down toward the earth has to elicit "ooh"s and "ah"s. Challenge your students to recreate these exciting explosions of color in the activity below.

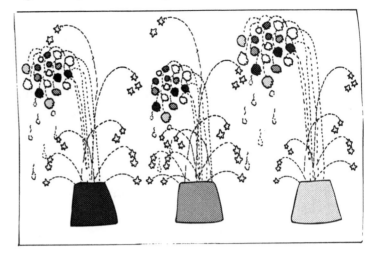

Materials:
- 12" x 18" (30.5 x 45.7 cm) sheet of dark blue construction paper
- 3" (7.5 cm) squares of construction paper in bright colors: red, yellow, pink, green
- saucers with different colors of tempera paint: red, white, pink, yellow
- one saucer with a puddle of white glue
- glitter
- small printing tools: pencil erasers, fingers, Q -Tips or sponge pieces
- paste

Steps to follow:

1. Set up a printing center. Arrange for two or three students to work at a time.

2. The class may begin this experiment by working at their individual desks with paper and paste. Give each student three squares of paper, one each of three different colors. Students trim the sides to create a cone shape and then they use the scraps to decorate the cones. Students paste the decorated cones to the bottom of their large blue construction paper.

3. At this point, students take turns going to the print center to add colorful fireworks to their picture. They need to experiment with several different techniques using the pencil erasers, fingers, etc., on newsprint before they do the actual printing on the blue construction paper. It is interesting to use both paint and sprinkled glitter on dots of glue.

Encourage students to experiment with different techniques.

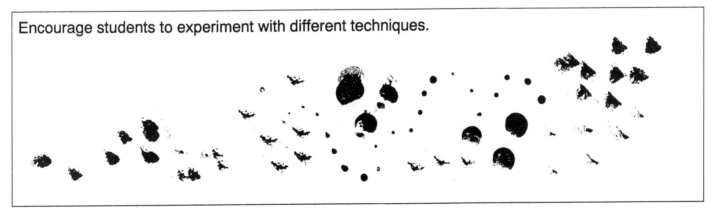

The Sunbather

Sitting in the summer sun may not be the best thing for our skins, but it's still fun to do. This sunbather is decked out in a broad-brimmed hat for some protection from the sun. Encourage your students to create colorful swimsuits and funny hats on their "cross-legged" sunbathers.

Materials:
- colored construction paper in a variety of skin colors 9" (22.8 cm) square for the body
- scissors, glue and crayons
- stapler
- a copy of the arm, head, hat and ball patterns on page 175
- assorted scraps of construction paper

Steps to follow:

1. Follow the basic folding directions with the 9" square piece of construction paper.

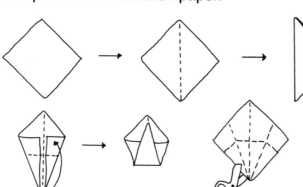

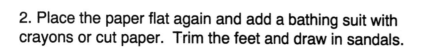

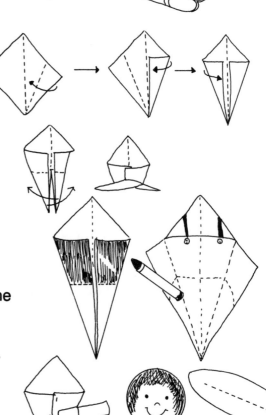

2. Place the paper flat again and add a bathing suit with crayons or cut paper. Trim the feet and draw in sandals.

3. Refold the paper and cross the sunbathers legs. Staple the legs together where they cross.

4. Cut out the head and arms using the pattern on page 175.

5. Glue on the head. Add hair and facial features using crayons or cut paper. Add a sunhat with a broad brim.

6. Glue the hands to the beach ball. Slip it over the top of the sunbather. Students may use the extra beach balls to tuck into the sunbather's pouch to record their favorite literature books, or to keep their spelling words or math facts to practice.

Seasonal Art

Sunbather Patterns

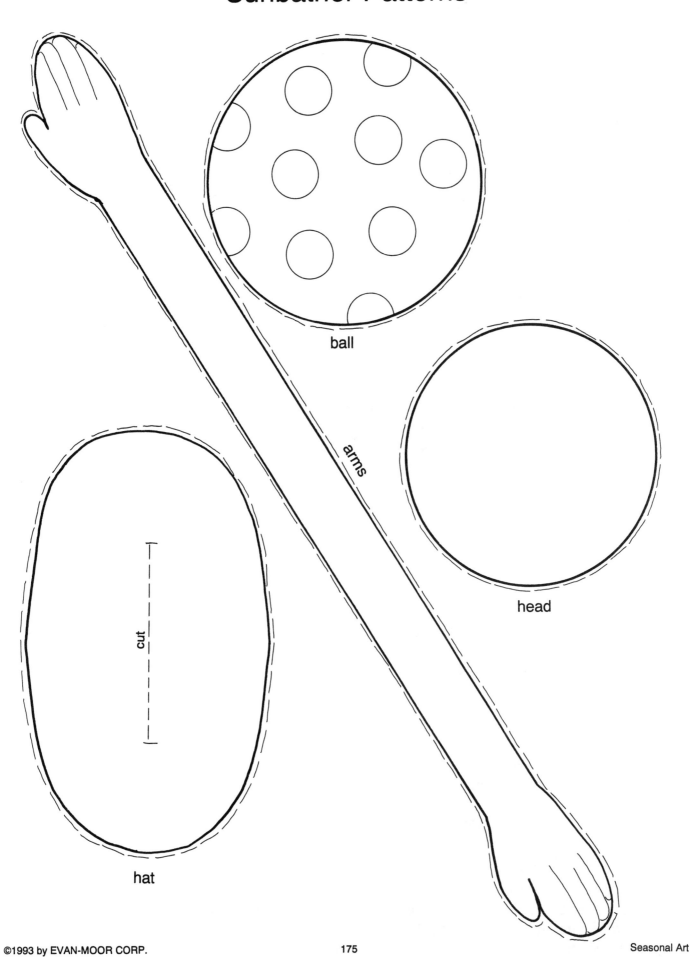

ball

arms

head

cut

hat

Seasonal Art

Memories of Summer

Memories can be stored in many ways. In this activity, children experience storing their memories of summer by making rubbings of the things they find in nature.

Materials:
- 12" x 18" (30.5 x 45.7 cm) sheets of white art paper
- paper fasteners or strips of yarn to fasten the pages together
- crayons in various colors with the paper wrappers removed
- collection of objects to use in making rubbings
- a large brown paper bag

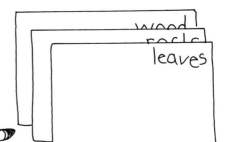

Steps to follow:

1. Each student gets several sheets of white art paper. Students label each one with a different category: leaves, rocks, wood, etc.

2. Throughout the summer as the student finds an interesting sample of one of these categories, he/she makes a rubbing of the item on the appropriate page. Encourage your students to overlap images and experiment with different color combinations.

3. At the end of the summer, create a brown paper bag cover for the rubbings. Fasten the pages together with paper fasteners or strips of yarn.

- Cut down the side of the bag.
- Cut out the bottom of the bag.
- Fold the bag in half.

   Your students may also enjoy adding written entries to record memorable events from their summer activities, perhaps explaining where and when they found the items in their rubbings scrapbooks.

 Seasonal Art

Buzzing Bees

Sitting under a tree on a lazy summer's day, you can hear the sounds of the birds and insects flying about. Here's a chance to make your own busy, buzzing bee.

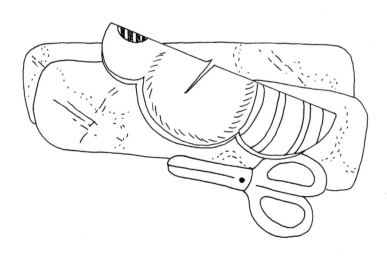

Materials:
- a copy of the bee pattern on page 178 (reproduce this on construction paper)
- wax paper for wings
- a dinner size paper plate
- 9 pieces of 4" x 3" (10 x 7.5 cm) yellow construction paper
- a puddle of red tempera paint in a plate
- small sponge squares
- scissors and glue

Steps to follow:

The Flower:

1. Sponge red paint onto the center of the paper plate.

2. Round the two corners of one end of each yellow rectangle.

Glue the yellow pieces to the outside of the paper plate creating the petals of a flower.

The Bee:

1. Color, cut and fold the bee pattern according to directions.

2. Cut two wings from wax paper. Pleat the wings in the center and slip into the slot in the bee's back.

3. Cut two antennae from paper scraps and glue to the head piece.

4. Set the bee in the center of the flower. Glue in place or pin up as a part of a bulletin board display.

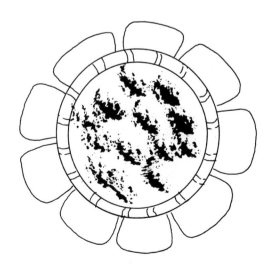

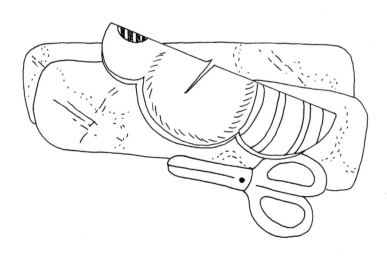

Seasonal Art

Bee Patterns

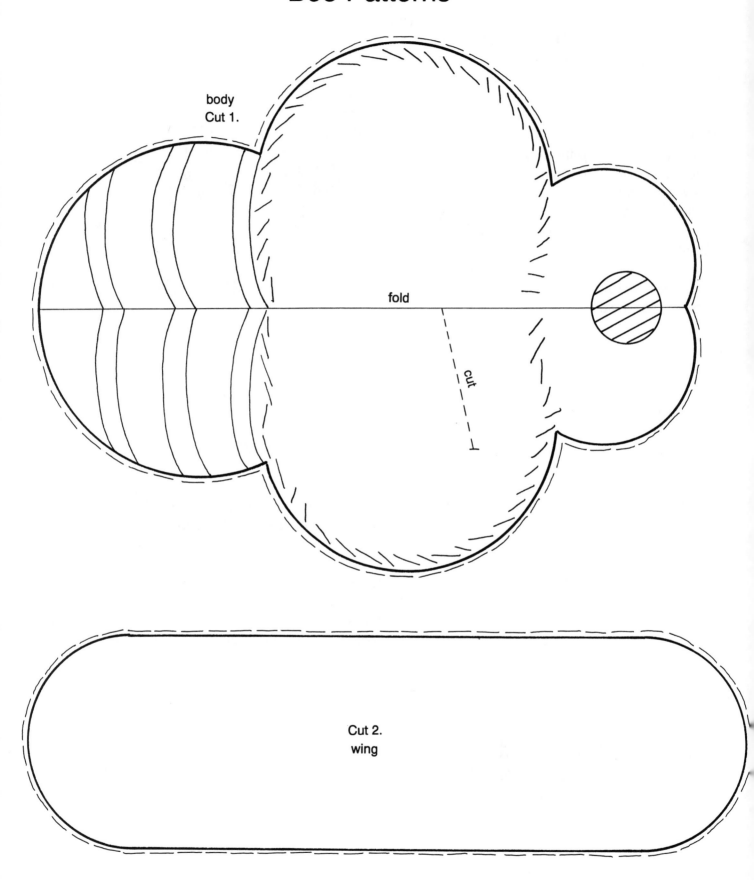

body
Cut 1.

fold

cut

Cut 2.
wing

Seasonal Art

Dancing Toy

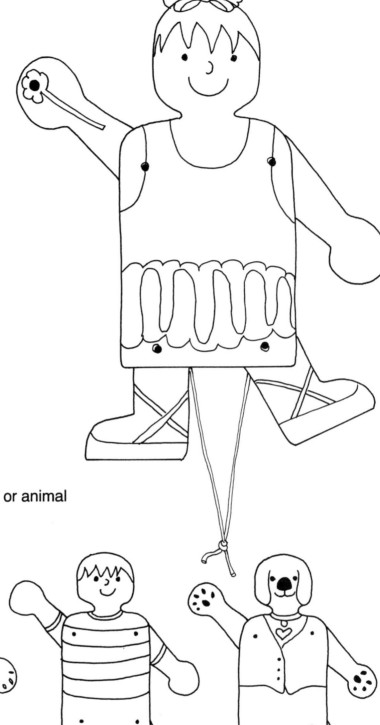

Summer is a great time for enjoying all of your toys and games. It can be even more fun making your own toys. This dancing toy is challenging to make and fun to play with.

Materials:
• patterns on pages 180 and 181
• 4 inches (10 cm) of string
• tagboard
• felt pens
• scissors and hole punch
• glue

Steps to follow:
1. Students may create any character or animal they wish on the pattern form.

2. Glue the patterns to tagboard. Cut out the shapes on the dotted lines.

3. Punch holes where indicated. Attach the body parts to each other with paper fasteners. Move them back and forth to increase ease of movement.

4. Thread the string through the holes as indicated on page 181.

Dancing Toy Pattern

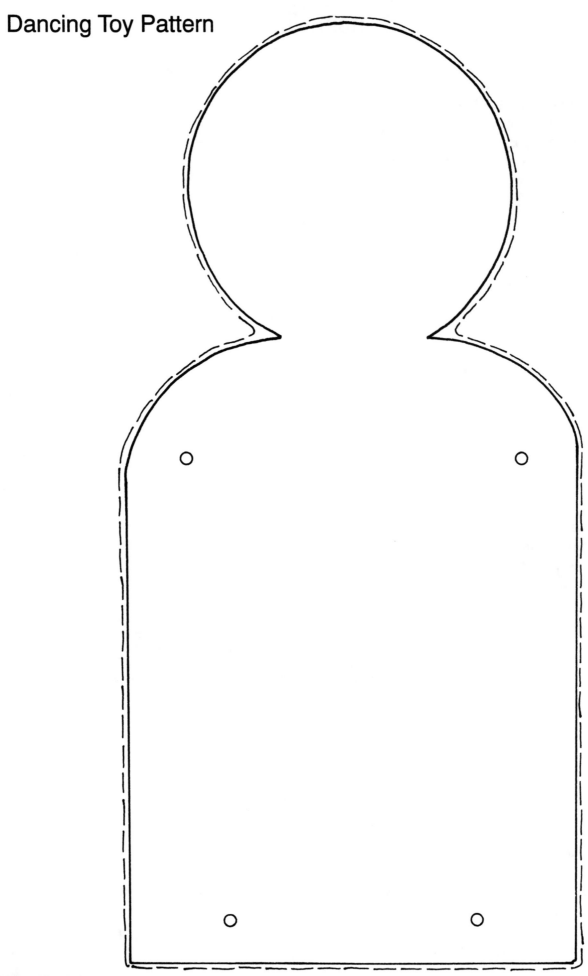

Seasonal Art

Dancing Toy Patterns (cont.)

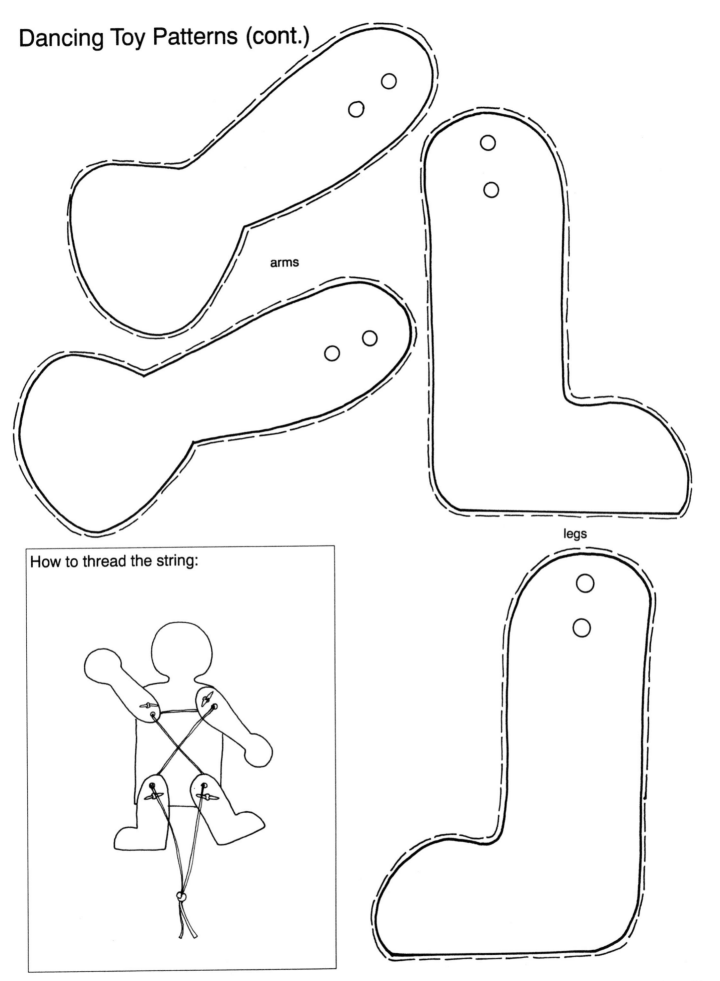

arms

legs

How to thread the string:

Seasonal Art

Spiral Shapes Mobile

Mobils are always a challenge. How DO you get them balanced? This one just requires you to "pull a few strings." Hang these where a gentle breeze blows and watch the spirals sway.

Materials:
• 6" (15 cm) squares in a variety of colors
• 2 straws
• string
• scissors
• a pencil
• hole punch

Steps to follow:

1. Draw the basic shapes (squares, triangles, ovals, circles) on different colored paper squares. Cut out the shapes.

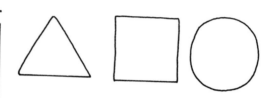

2. Lightly trace a spiral on each shape. Cut along the lines you have drawn.

3. Punch a hole in the center of each shape.

4. Cut the string into three- 24" (61 cm) lengths. Tie one of your spirals to one end of each of two strings.

5. Thread the other end of each string through a straw.

6. Now tie a spiral shape to the other end of each string.

7. Place the straws across one another at right angles. Tie the two straws together at the center point with your remaining piece of string.

8. Hang up the mobile. Balance it by pulling the strings back and forth through the straws.

Seasonal Art

Origami Snake

Always watch where you are going when you're out hiking in rocky, wooded areas on those hot summer days. You don't want to accidentally disturb a snake's naptime! You won't have to worry about this origami snake. It will stay wherever you happen to put it.

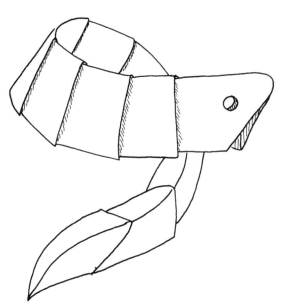

Materials:
• long strip of 3" (7.5 cm) wide shelf or wrapping paper (the longer the paper, the longer the snake)
• hole punch
• scissors
• a ruler and pencil
• paste
• crayons or felt pens

Steps to follow:
1. Fold the paper in half the long way. Add colorful designs with crayon or felt pen.

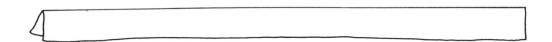

2. Opening the paper flat again, begin making pleats about 3" (7.5 cm) from the end of the paper. Continue making pleats within the last 3" (7.5 cm) of the end. Refold the snake in half the long way.

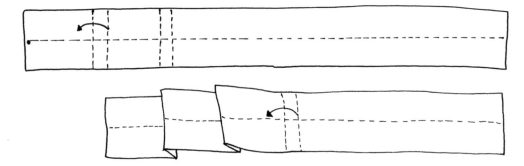

3. Round the edges of one end for the snake's head. Use a hole punch for the eye.

4. Cut the other end to a point for the tail.

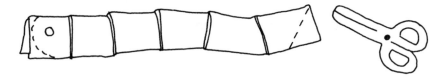

Seasonal Art

Dragonfly Flyer

Why do you suppose they are called dragonflies?
Sit quietly and you might see this interesting
fellow passing by. Even though they have fragile—
looking wings, dragonflies are great fliers. Make
your own dragonfly to soar about outside.

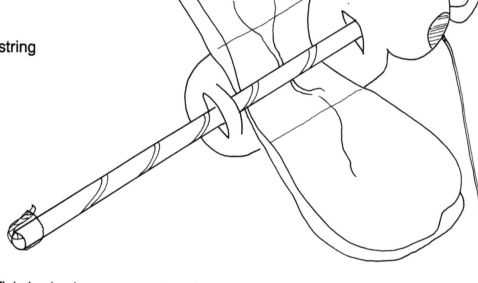

Materials:
- a copy of the wing and body patterns
  on page 185
- a plastic drinking straw
- wax paper
- 2 yards (183 meters) of string
- scissors
- tape

Steps to follow:

1. Reproduce the dragonfly's body shape on construction
paper. Color and cut it out. Also cut the slit lines on the back.

2. Cut two wings from wax paper according to the pattern.

3. Slip the straw through the slits on the back of the dragonfly.
Tape the end of the straw behind the dragonfly's head.

4. Crinkle up the wax paper wings. Put the wings together and
slip them under the straw.

5. Thread the string through the straw. Secure the string with
tape at the back end of the straw.

6. Fold dragonfly's feet down and curl his antennae around a
pencil.

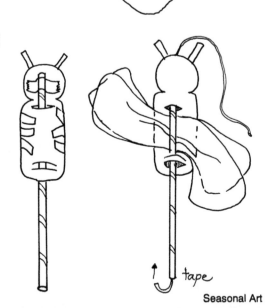

tape

Seasonal Art

Dragonfly Patterns

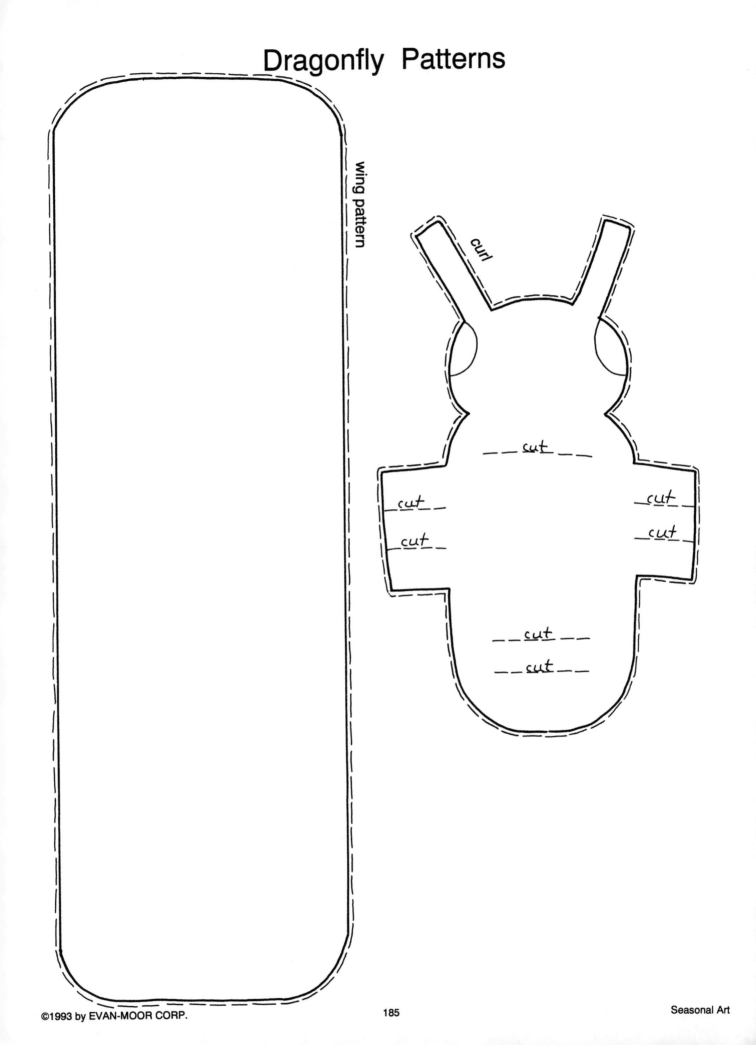

wing pattern

curl

cut

cut

cut

cut

cut

cut

cut

Seasonal Art

Paper Chain of Inner-Tube Swimmers

Cutting paper chains seems to be a lost art. Creating this delightful chain of bubbly inner-tube swimmers may be just the thing to get your students started experimenting with chains of their own.

Materials:
- a copy of the pattern on this page cut out of tagboard
- long sheets of lightweight paper for folding and cutting the paper chain (newspaper, shelf paper, duplicator paper, etc.)
- crayons or felt pens
- scissors

Steps to follow:

1. Mark the paper off into 3" (7.5 cm) segments. Accordion-fold the paper at these segments.

2. Trace the pattern on the first segment.

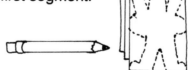

3. Cut through all the segments on the pattern line. Do not cut all the way around the inner-tube line because that is what ties all the swimmers together.

4. Students add details with their felt pens or crayons. Each swimmer may be done differently to add interest.

These chains can be pinned around the edges of bulletin boards to create a great summer border.

pattern

Do not cut!

Do not cut!

Seasonal Art

Forest Animal Pinch-and-Tear Pictures

How do you make a furry animal look furry? This can be challenging especially when you are using construction paper. This activity allows children to achieve "furry" animals by tearing the outside shape, leaving a rough, uneven edge. After a little practice, they can create a whole forest full of furry friends.

Materials:
- 12" x 18" (30.5 x 45.7 cm) green construction paper
- 6" (15 cm) squares of brown construction paper
- scraps of construction paper for details
- a black felt pen
- paste

Steps to follow:

1. Draw (on the chalkboard) some of the forest animal shapes students might choose to make. Several animals based on simple shapes are given below to help you get started.

2. Give each student several brown construction paper squares. Have them lightly draw the shapes they need for their animal on the square. Then they pinch and tear out each of the shapes. Lay the shapes together to create the animal pictures. Encourage students to experiment and lay different shapes together to create new animal forms.

3. After students have experimented making several animals, they may paste their creatures to the green construction paper.

Note: You aren't really doing this lesson correctly unless you create a huge pile of torn paper scraps to sift through. All kinds of new animals can be discovered hiding in those scraps!

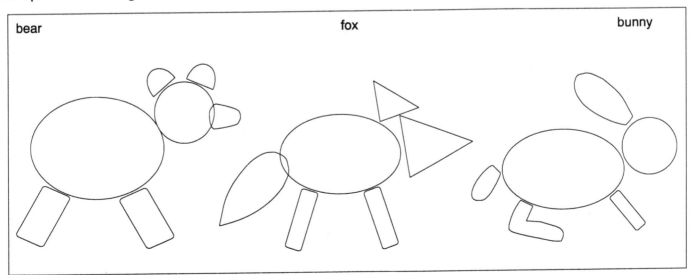

bear   fox   bunny

187   Seasonal Art

By the Sea, By the Sea

Swimming or surfing or just lying in the sun...there's no better way to spend a hot summer's day than romping or resting at the beach. Here is a chance to recreate that experience on paper.

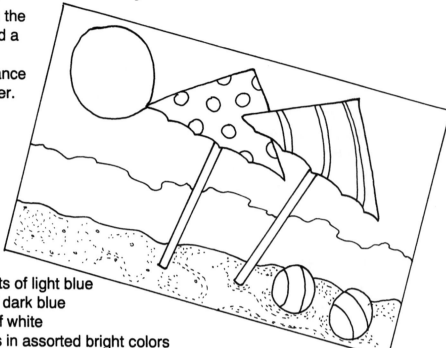

Materials:
• construction paper
    12" x 18" (30.5 x 45.7 cm) sheets of light blue
    6" x 18" (15 x 45.7 cm) sheet of dark blue
    3" x 18" (7.5 x 45.7 cm) sheet of white
    9" x 12" (22.8 x 30.5 cm) sheets in assorted bright colors
• the umbrella patterns on page 189 to trace around
• watered-down white glue
• a paint brush
• sand
• felt pens
• paste and scissors

Steps to follow:

1. Rip one edge off the **dark** blue construction paper. Paste this sheet to the bottom half of the **light** blue construction paper.

2. Cut a curved line on the edge of the white construction paper. Paste it to the bottom of the blue construction paper.

3. Paint the white strip with watered-down white glue. Sprinkle sand over this area to create a sandy beach. Dump off the excess sand and set the paper aside to dry.

4. Cut out umbrellas, beach balls and a sun from brightly colored construction paper. Encourage students to add stripes, polka-dots, and other details to their work with felt pens.

5. Arrange the umbrellas and balls on the "sandy" beach of the blue paper. Will the beach balls be bobbing on the water or resting on the sand? Paste the shapes in place.

Umbrella Patterns

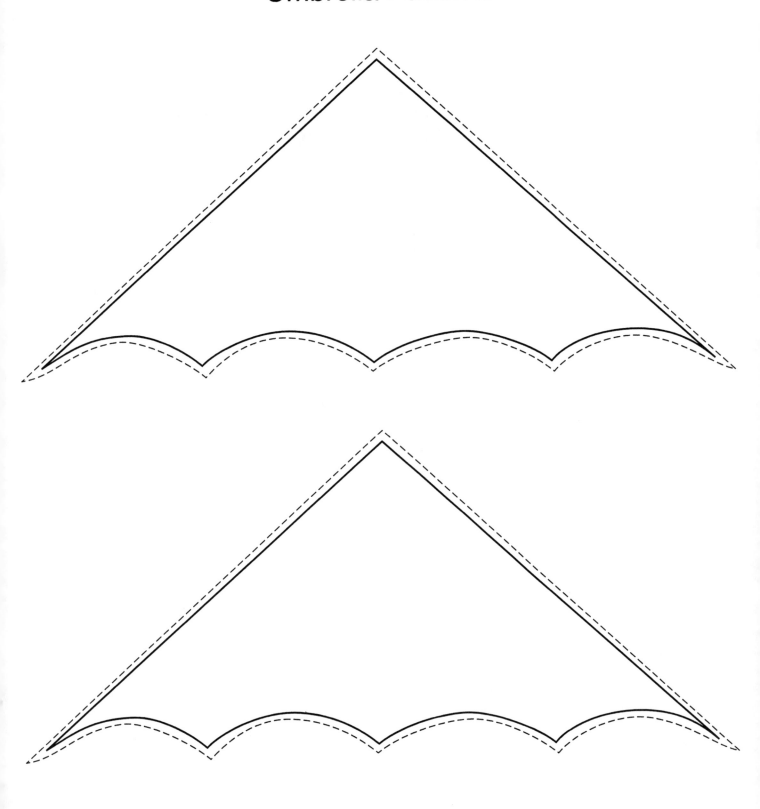

Seasonal Art

Summer Sponge Painting Fun

All the warmth of summer seems wrapped up in these colorful sponge paintings The rough texture of the sponges adds interest to the final prints. Provide time for experimentation before creating final projects.

Materials:
• tempera paint in yellow, orange, red and magenta
• saucers or lids to hold paint for printing
• sponge pieces cut in shapes (See page 191.)
• 12" x 18" (30.5 x 45.7 cm) sheets of white art paper
• felt pens
• newspaper

Steps to follow:

1. Cut sponges into shapes. You may use scissors or Exacto knives to get a smooth cut line.

2. Pour puddles of paint in saucers and dip in sponges. Students should practice printing with the sponges on newspaper until they learn just how much paint needs to be on the sponge to get a clear print. They may also want to experiment with the different shapes and combinations they can make.

3. When they are ready, have students create a final design on the white art paper.

4. After the paint dries, details may be added with felt pens.

Seasonal Art

Sample Sponge Shapes

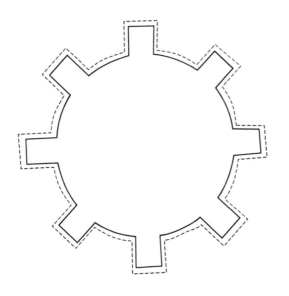

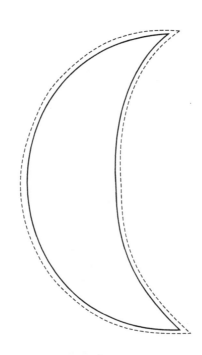

Seasonal Art

Early Bird Catches the Worm

With a flock of these "early birds" around, you certainly don't want to be a plump worm.

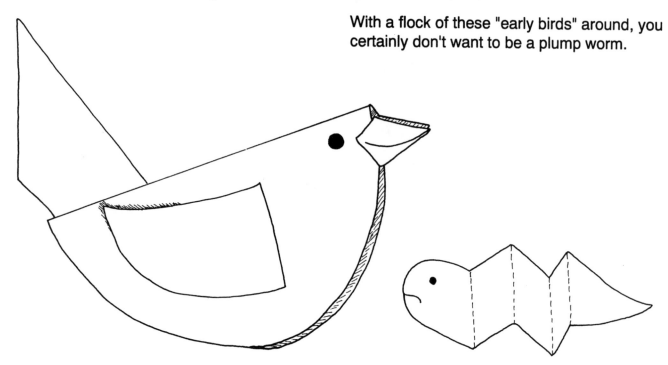

Materials:
- a copy of the pattern on page 193 reproduced on tagboard
- construction paper
- scissors
- paste
- felt pens

Steps to follow:
1. Color and cut out the patterns on page 193.

2. Fold the circle for the bird in half.

3. Paste the beak parts together.
Add on the tail and wings.

4. Add an eye and other details with felt pens.

5. Fold the worm like an accordion. Add details with felt pens.

6. Set both animals on the table and think about what they might be saying to one another.

     Seasonal Art

Bird and Worm Patterns

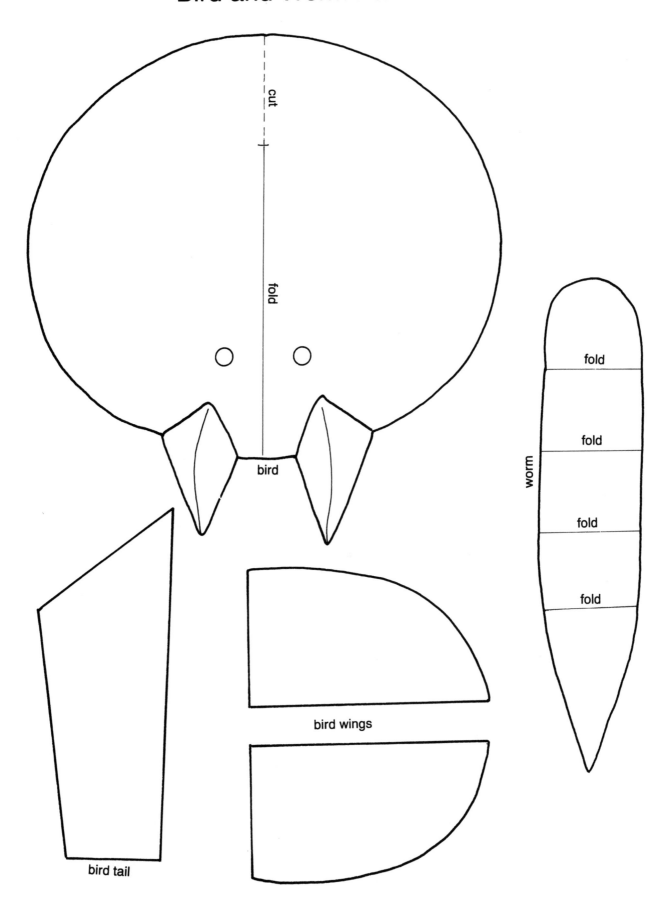

cut

fold

bird

worm

fold

fold

fold

fold

bird wings

bird tail

Seasonal Art

My Father and Me
a portrait

Materials:
- large paint paper
- wide and pointed tempera brushes
- a 2" (5 cm) wide brush
- tempera paint in several colors
- watered-down white glue
- glitter
- a pencil and eraser

Steps to follow:

1. Students lightly draw their fathers and themselves on the paint paper. They may choose to do a portrait of the full body or just the face and shoulders. Encourage them to draw large and fill the paper. This drawing should be just an outline. They will add details on the paint layer.

2. Then they paint over the pencil lines and add color. Now is the time to add as much detail as they wish. Can anything be seen in the background? If so, is it the interior of a house or is it somewhere outdoors?

3. After the paint dies, mix white glue with water and use a wide brush (house-paint variety) to apply a thin coat over the entire picture. Allow this layer to dry and then repeat.

4, Before the last layer of glue dries (the more layers, the shinier it will be), sprinkle glitter around the outside edge to create a sparkling frame.

Seasonal Art

Crickets Mean Good Luck

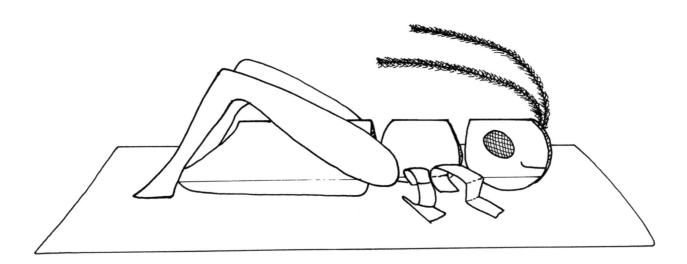

The wonderful sound of crickets chirping through the night can never be forgotten. Here is an activity that can be used to introduce a science class to how crickets make their sound or just as an opportunity to have fun creating three-dimensional insects. Either way, you've already had "good luck"!

Materials:
• a copy of the pattern on page 196 run on construction paper
• a pipe cleaner
• 9" x 12" (22.8 x 30.5 cm) sheet of construction paper
• construction paper scraps for adding detail
• felt pens
• white glue

Steps to follow:
1. Color and cut out the cricket pattern.

2. Follow the folding directions.

3. Glue the cricket to the 9" x 12" (22.8 x 30.5 cm) sheet of construction paper. Glue each segment so that there is some space between.

4. Fold the pipe cleaner in half and put a spot of glue on the folded end. Slip the glued end into the folded section of the head segment.

5. Glue the back legs in place on each side of the back segment.

6. Fold and paste the other four legs by the center segment.

 Seasonal Art

Cricket Pattern

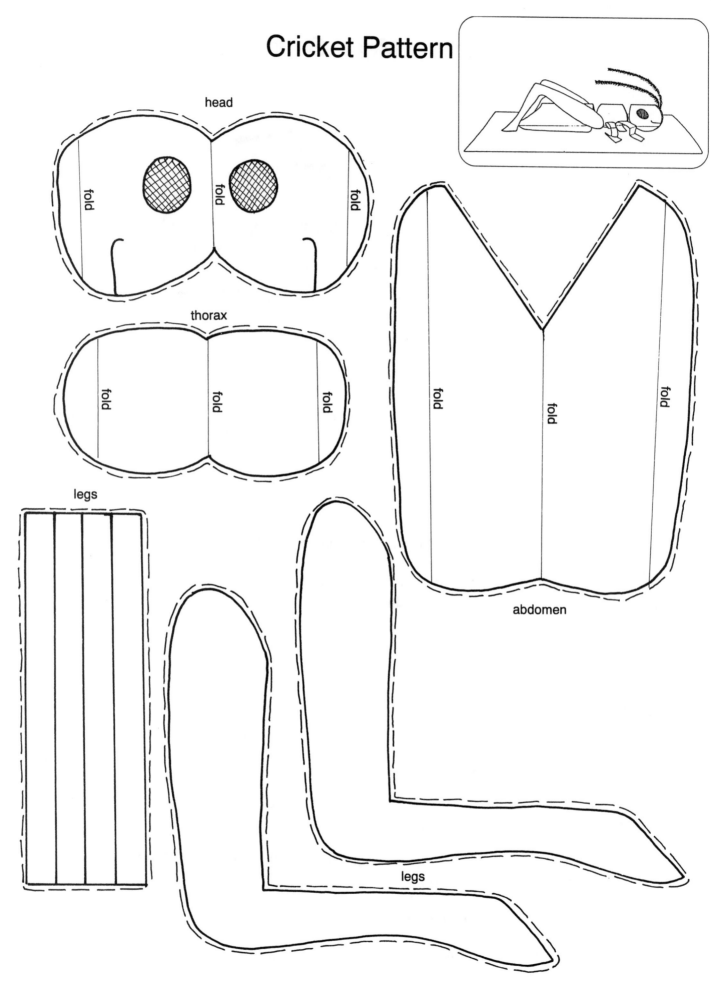

head

thorax

legs

fold

abdomen

legs

Seasonal Art

At the Pond

Did you ever splash around in a pond looking for tadpoles and little fish? Or tried to catch hopping frogs? Or sat quietly watching the water birds? Here is an opportunity to recreate that atmosphere of cool water, green plants and blue sky on a sunny summer's afternoon.

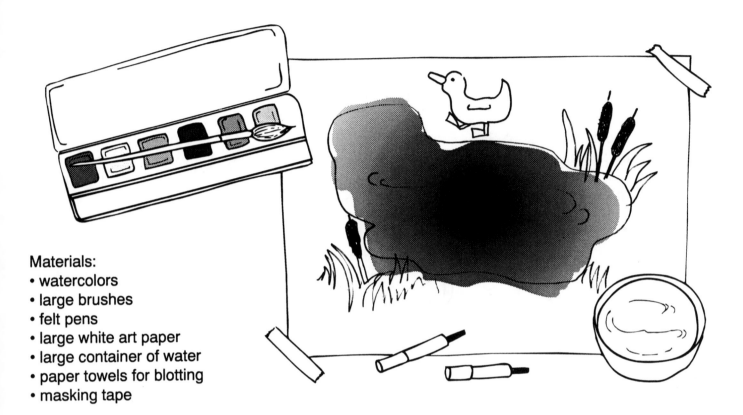

Materials:
• watercolors
• large brushes
• felt pens
• large white art paper
• large container of water
• paper towels for blotting
• masking tape

Steps to follow:

1. Discuss what one might see at a pond: water, tall grass, cattails, ducks, frogs and maybe even a thirsty fox?

2. Tape the corners of the paper securely to the table. Experiment with doing a light blue wash over the entire surface of the paper. Swish water around on the paper first and then fill the brush with the blue watercolor. Leave puddles of color. Create a mottled effect on the entire sheet. Allow this layer to dry.

3. Think about your composition now. Which area will remain sky, where will the pond fit? How much grass will show? Are there going to be animals in this picture?

4. Now add a layer of darker blue watercolor in the area that will be the pond. Students may want to mix in some purple as well to create more contrast. Allow this layer to dry.

5. Use the greens on your watercolor tray to create the grassy area around the pond. Try mixing your green with blue or yellow to change its hue. Students may use a watery wash effect or they may want to experiment with a dry brush effect doing separate lines approximating grass and weeds. Allow this layer to dry.

6. Draw in with felt pen the animals or other details in your picture. Students may also wish to do outlining of the items in the picture to create a more structured effect.

 Seasonal Art

My Campout Diorama

Sittting around a campfire in the evening after the sun has set brings wonderful new sensations to mind. What is causing that rustling sound in the underbrush? What plant or animal is that you smell? What just flew overhead? Add to this the sounds and smells of the campfire. Encourage students to share experiences about camping out. If no one has camped out, encourage them to draw on stories and movies to create an imaginary campsite. This is a good activity for working in partners.

Materials:
• a shoe box
• sample diorama patterns on page 199
• a selection of construction paper colors and scraps
• scissors
• white glue
• a "junk supply" box of egg cartons, pipe cleaners, etc.
• tempera paint and brushes

My Camp
tent
camp fire
bear
stream
birds

Steps to follow:
1. Have students work with a partner to build a camp scene.   The first thing they need to do is to create a list of all the things that might exist in this scene: tents, campfire, trees, a stream, firewood, birds and perhaps even a bear?

2. Students begin by painting the inside of their box with tempera paint. They need to have a plan about how the paint will show the sky, the land, etc.

3. After the paint is dry, the students complete their scene from construction paper and "junk" supplies, using white glue to place the items permanently in the box.

4. Have children give a title to their finished diorama. Students may write the title and their own names on a small flap of construction paper. Glue the sign to the top of the diorama.

Seasonal Art

Diorama Patterns

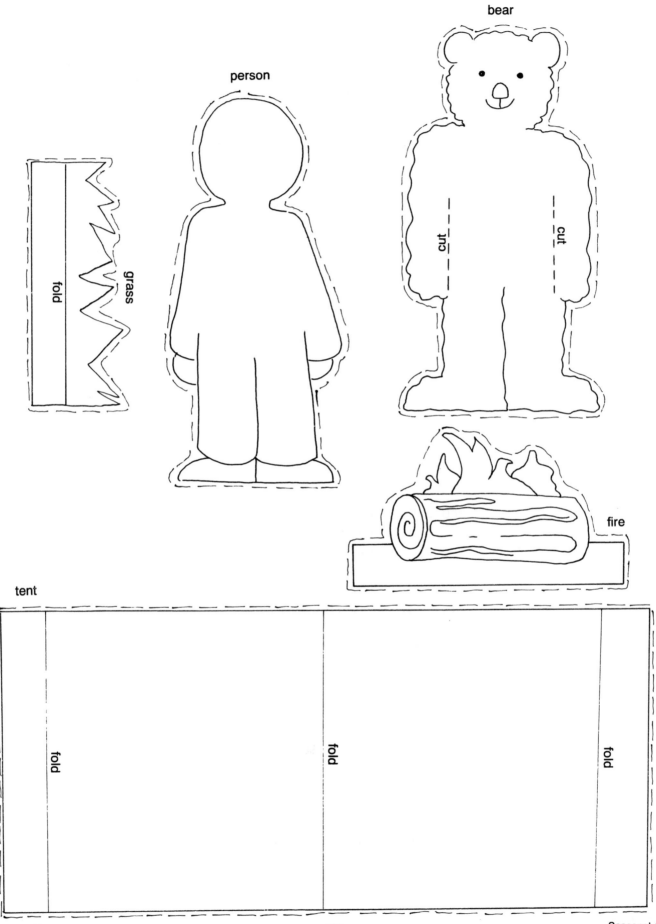

bear

person

grass

fold

cut

cut

fire

tent

fold

fold

fold

Seasonal Art

Weaving from Nature

Begin this activity by taking a class walking trip to collect natural items to add to the weavings. Explore possibilities with your students. Challenge them to come up with creative solutions to problems that might arise. For example, how can you keep your weaving still while you work? What do you do if you run out of yarn in the middle of a row? How can you incorporate a special piece of bark or moss in your weaving? The finished projects should be displayed in a hallway or the library for everyone to admire.

Materials:
• twigs and small branches
• string
• a collection of yarns
• weeds, grasses, bark moss
• scissors
• tape

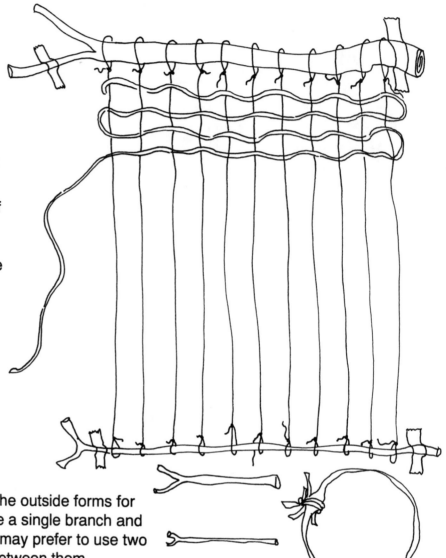

Steps to follow:
 1. Pick which branches will become the outside forms for your weaving. You may choose to use a single branch and bend it into a circle. Or your students may prefer to use two branches as end pieces and weave between them.

2. Tie a long length of string to the branch. Wrap the string around to create the lines on which you will weave. A weaver calls this the *warp*. If you are using two separate branches, you will need to tape them to a table so that the lines remain stretched and tight.

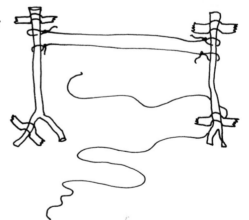

3. Now begins the fun. You may begin weaving yarns or strips of grass or moss in and out of your warp lines. Gently pull down each line you weave to the bottom of the weaving area. Keep adding line after line until the area is full. You may change yarns at any time by tying the yarn off to a warp line when you are ready to add a new color or texture. Remember, open areas can be very attractive in this type of weaving.

         Seasonal Art

Welcome Summer Banner

There is nothing like wiggling your toes in something cool on a hot summer day. So combine a cool wiggle for your feet in tempera paint and a chance to create a colorful display to put up and enjoy each day. Don't forget to have a generous supply of paper towels, soap and water on hand for clean-up once those feet have walked through the paint.

Materials:
• a roll of shelf paper
• tempera paint in primary colors: red, yellow and blue
• brushes
• pie plates
• newspaper and paper towels

Steps to follow:
1. Roll out a long sheet of shelf paper. Tape the corners to the floor. Decide on a message to print on the banner. The message may be long or it can come right to the point, such as...Welcome Summer. Sketch out the message lightly on the banner with a pencil.

2. Give each student a letter in the message to design. They may use tempera paint and brushes or felt pens.

3. Place puddles of the tempera paint in separate pie plates and smear to cover the bottom of the plates. Students remove shoes and socks and press both of their feet into the pie plates. Then they step onto the banner and walk. Use this technique with each of the three primary colors. Have a dishpan of soapy water and lots of paper towels handy to facilitate the clean-up of all those paint smeared feet.

   Seasonal Art

Paper Strip Art

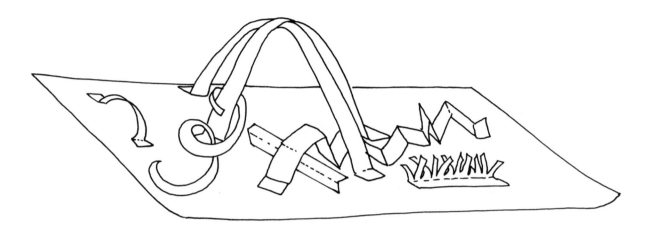

Offer students the opportunity to create 3-dimensional pieces of art from flat paper. Encourage them to experiment with several techniques of paper folding, bending and twisting that can be used together to build "paper sculptures."

Materials:
• a handful of 1" x 18" (2.5 x 45.7 cm) construction paper strips in bright colors
• 12" x 18" (30.5 x 45.7 cm) sheet of construction paper in a contrasting color
• paste
• scissors

Steps to follow:
1. Place the large sheet of construction paper on the table as a base for the art work. Glue the paper strips to this base. Try different techniques of paper folding, curling, and cutting and scoring with each new strip you add.

2. As each strip is glued to the base, experiment with ways of intertwining and bending strips to create a 3-dimensional effect.

3. The finished "sculpture" of paper strips may by pinned on a bulletin board for a colorful and textured display.

 Seasonal Art

Suggested paper strip techniques to share with students:

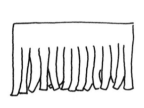

curl

fold

bend

fringe

cut spiral

pleat

Seasonal Art

Shoe Box Characters

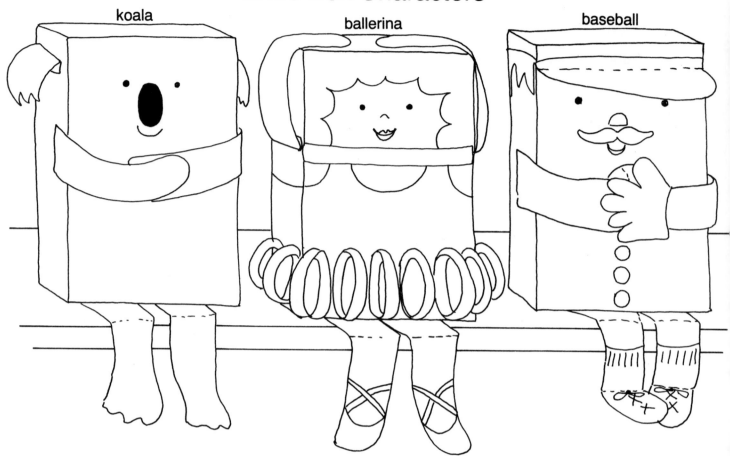

koala　　　　ballerina　　　　baseball

Create characters from storybooks or characters from real life. Use leftover shoe boxes to develop a wonderful display of student work. Invite your class to use paper, paint and fabric bits to build these characters using creative techniques.

Materials:
• shoe boxes
• cloth remnants, yarn, tissue paper, string, construction paper,
  wallpaper and other paper choices
• glue
• felt pens
• tempera paint and brushes

Steps to follow:
1. Paint the shoe boxes.

2. Students may use the paper scraps, yarn, etc., to create the box character they visualize. Encourage students to experiment with different possibilities. They may change their minds if they discover one plan doesn't work.

3. Set the box characters on a shelf as they are completed so that students can see how many different characters and techniques were used.

 Seasonal Art

Gone Fishing

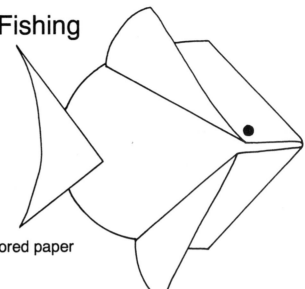

Create origami fish and display on a bulletin board along with tales of summer fun. Students may enjoy making a whole school of fish in different colors and designs.

Materials:
• 5" (13 cm) or 8" (20.5 cm) squares of brightly colored paper
• scissors
• felt pens or crayons
• string (for hanging up)

Steps to follow:
1. Fold the square. Hold on to the folded tip and round off the open tip.

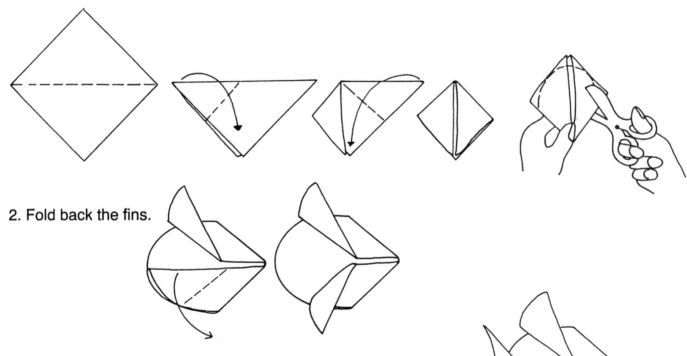

2. Fold back the fins.

3. Reverse the cut-off tip of paper and paste it onto the fish as a tail.

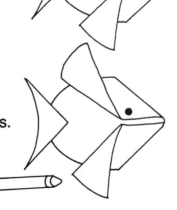

4. Add an eye with felt pen or crayon.
You may also add polka-dots, stripes or other decorative features.

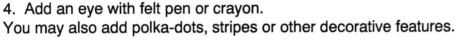

 Seasonal Art

Frog at the Pond

Have your students caught any frogs this summer? Build on their stories of summer fun around the pond by making these frogs. Everyone can share the adventure when they have their own pop-up frog.

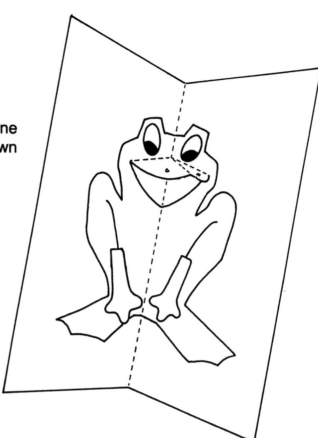

Materials:
• a copy of the patterns on pages 207 and 208
• crayons
• scissors
• a sheet of 8 1/2" x 11" (21.6 x 28 cm) construction paper

Steps to follow:
1. Color the body parts.

2. Cut on the outside lines.

3. Body:
   a. Fold the body in half on fold 1. The colored side should be on the outside.

   b. Cut the mouth line while folded in half.

   c. Fold line 2 while folded in half. Fold each line away from you and then again towards you.

   d. Unfold the body. Push the mouth up between the eyes until the frog folds flat.

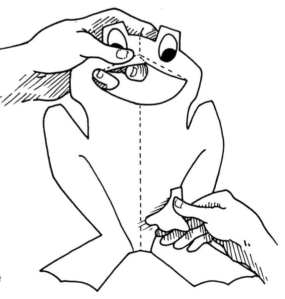

4. Glue the frog to the 8 1/2" x 11" construction paper. Apply glue only to the frog's body, not to his mouth. Glue the front feet in place. Students may add their own background design to the paper.

       Seasonal Art

Frog Pattern

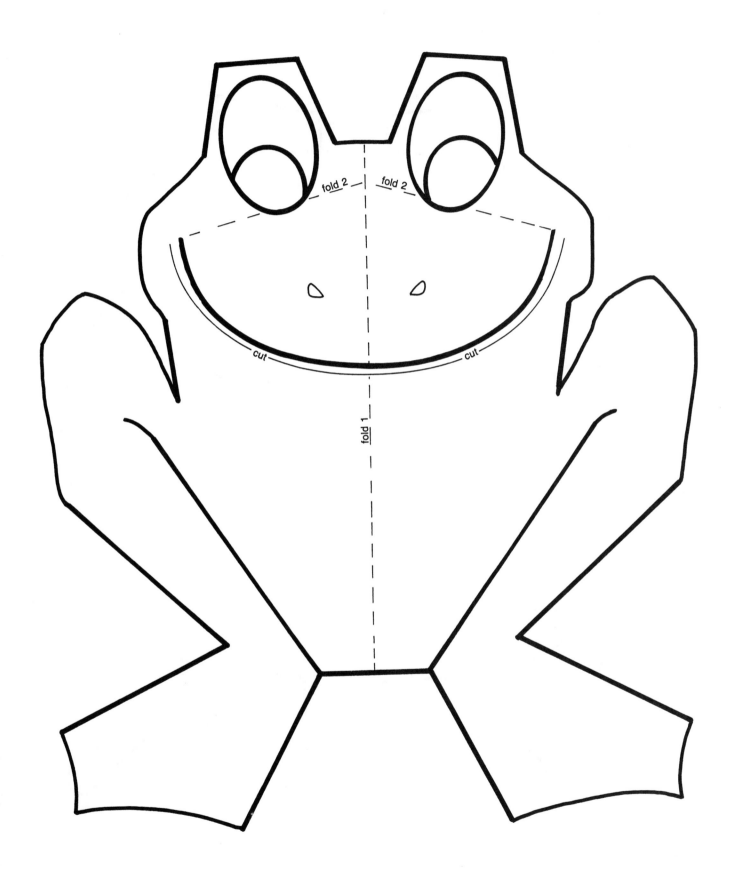

fold 2 — fold 2

cut   cut

fold 1

Seasonal Art

Frog Front Feet

Each student will need two frog feet.

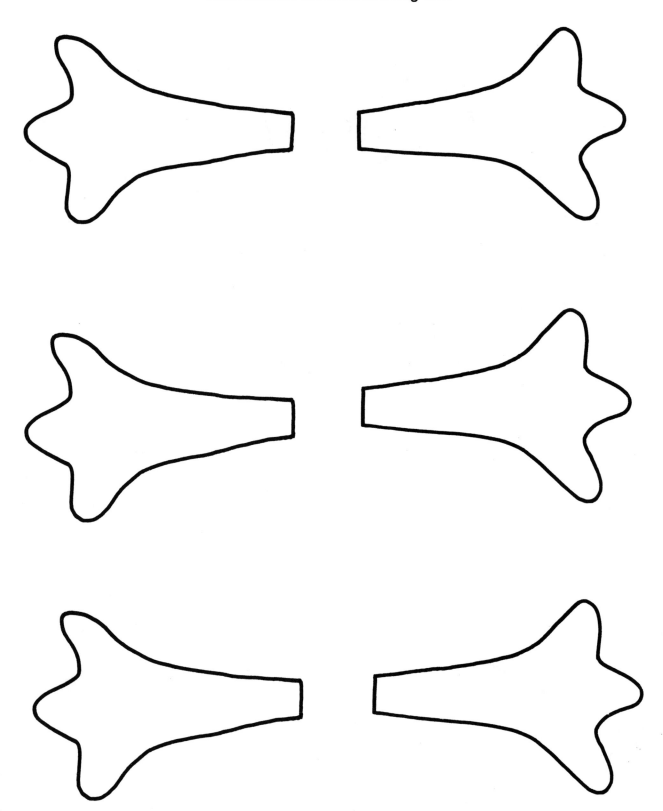

Seasonal Art